James A. Marley, PhD

Family Involvement in Treating Schizophrenia
Models, Essential Skills, and Process

Pre-publication
REVIEWS,
COMMENTARIES,
EVALUATIONS . . .

"James Marley has performed a remarkable feat in abstracting some useful techniques from discredited theories of schizophrenia. The research-supported section on multiple family groups, behavioral family therapy, and psychoeducational interventions will be of considerable value to family therapists trained in older conceptual models."

Harriet P. Lefley, PhD
Professor of Psychiatry
and Behavioral Sciences,
University of Miami School of Medicine

"This is a very important book. It is the first book on family therapy that I have seen that adequately addresses both the strengths and limitations of current family therapy models with respect to families of people with serious mental illnesses. This book should be required reading for all family therapy professionals who work with families of people with serious mental illnesses. Marley correctly assumes that families do not cause mental illnesses and that their primary need is for information, coping skills, and support. He also addresses the importance of self-help for families and for those teaching other families about mental illnesses."

Le Roy Spaniol, PhD
Executive Publisher,
Psychiatric Rehabilitation Journal

More pre-publication
REVIEWS, COMMENTARIES, EVALUATIONS . . .

"This text is a must-read for every clinician involved in treating schizophrenia. This highly readable and well-organized book goes beyond the traditional psychoeducational and behavioral approaches to treating schizophrenia. Dr. Marley provides a comprehensive overview of a wide range of family therapy approaches for helping individuals and families struggling with schizophrenia. For each model, he provides an excellent overview of the core elements of the model, an outline of essential skills and techniques, and an illustration of the process of family therapy using the model. Throughout the text, he builds a strong case for the importance of family involvement in the treatment of schizophrenia, and for the value of a family-focused treatment approach.

The chapter on families and schizophrenia provides a solid developmental framework for understanding the impact of schizophrenia on all aspects of the family life cycle. There is also an excellent chapter summarizing the current state of the art in family therapy research on schizophrenia. The final chapter, 'Future Development,' raises a number of critical issues including the importance of avoiding reductionistic biological treatment approaches that fail to recognize the basic humanity of the individual and the importance of the environmental, cultural, and family contexts in which schizophrenia occurs and is treated. This book represents a significant contribution to the literature on family treatment of serious mental illnesses."

Malcolm M. MacFarlane, MA
Editor, *Family Therapy and Mental Health: Innovations in Theory and Practice*
and *Family Treatment of Personality Disorders: Advances in Clinical Practice;*
Section Editor,
Journal of Family Psychotherapy

The Haworth Clinical Practice Press
An Imprint of The Haworth Press, Inc.
New York • London • Oxford

NOTES FOR PROFESSIONAL LIBRARIANS AND LIBRARY USERS

This is an original book title published by The Haworth Clinical Practice Press, an imprint of The Haworth Press, Inc. Unless otherwise noted in specific chapters with attribution, materials in this book have not been previously published elsewhere in any format or language.

CONSERVATION AND PRESERVATION NOTES

All books published by The Haworth Press, Inc. and its imprints are printed on certified pH neutral, acid free book grade paper. This paper meets the minimum requirements of American National Standard for Information Sciences-Permanence of Paper for Printed Material, ANSI Z39.48-1984.

Family Involvement in Treating Schizophrenia
Models, Essential Skills, and Process

HAWORTH Marriage and the Family
Terry S. Trepper, PhD
Executive Editor

Couples Therapy, Second Edition by Linda Berg-Cross

Family Therapy and Mental Health: Innovations in Theory and Practice by Malcolm M. MacFarlane

How to Work with Sex Offenders: A Handbook for Criminal Justice, Human Service, and Mental Health Professionals by Rudy Flora

Marital and Sexual Lifestyles in the United States: Attitudes, Behaviors, and Relationships in Social Context by Linda P. Rouse

Psychotherapy with People in the Arts: Nurturing Creativity by Gerald Schoenewolf

Critical Incidents in Marital and Family Therapy: A Practitioner's Guide by David A. Baptiste Jr.

Clinical and Educational Interventions with Fathers edited by Jay Fagan and Alan J. Hawkins

Family Solutions for Substance Abuse: Clinical and Counseling Approaches by Eric E. McCollum and Terry S. Trepper

The Therapist's Notebook for Families: Solution-Oriented Exercises for Working with Parents, Children, and Adolescents by Bob Bertolino and Gary Schultheis

Between Fathers and Sons: Critical Incident Narratives in the Development of Men's Lives by Robert J. Pellegrini and Theodore R. Sarbin

Women's Stories of Divorce at Childbirth: When the Baby Rocks the Cradle by Hilary Hoge

Treating Marital Stress: Support-Based Approaches by Robert P. Rugel

An Introduction to Marriage and Family Therapy by Lorna L. Hecker and Joseph L. Wetchler

Solution-Focused Brief Therapy: Its Effective Use in Agency Settings by Teri Pichot and Yvonne M. Dolan

Becoming a Solution Detective: Identifying Your Client's Strengths in Practical Brief Therapy by John Sharry, Brendan Madden, and Melissa Darmody

Emotional Cutoff: Bowen Family Systems Theory Perspectives edited by Peter Titelman

Welcome Home! An International and Nontraditional Adoption Reader edited by Lita Linzer Schwartz and Florence W. Kaslow

Creativity in Psychotherapy: Reaching New Heights with Individuals, Couples, and Families by David K. Carson and Kent W. Becker

Understanding and Treating Schizophrenia: Contemporary Research, Theory and Practice by Glenn D. Shean

Family Involvement in Treating Schizophrenia: Models, Essential Skills, and Process by James A. Marley

Transgender Emergence: Therapeutic Guidelines for Working with Gender-Variant People and Their Families by Arlene Istar Lev

Family Treatment of Personality Disorders: Advances in Clinical Practice edited by Malcolm M. MacFarlane

Family Involvement in Treating Schizophrenia
Models, Essential Skills, and Process

James A. Marley, PhD

The Haworth Clinical Practice Press
An Imprint of The Haworth Press, Inc.
New York • London • Oxford

Published by

The Haworth Clinical Practice Press, an imprint of The Haworth Press, Inc., 10 Alice Street, Binghamton, NY 13904-1580.

Cover design by Jennifer M. Gaska.

Library of Congress Cataloging-in-Publication Data

Marley, James A.
Family involvement in treating schizophrenia : models, essential skills, and process / James A. Marley.
p. cm.
Includes bibliographical references and index.
ISBN 0-7890-1249-9 (alk. paper)—ISBN 0-7890-1250-2 (pbk. : alk. paper)
1. Schizophrenics—Family relationships. 2. Family psychotherapy. I. Title.
RC514 .M356 2003
616.89'82—dc21

2002154813

To my parents, Dick and Charlene, thank you for everything;
To my daughter, Eliza, who makes each day an adventure;
and to my wife, Leslie, whose love and support
make all things possible.

ABOUT THE AUTHOR

James A. Marley, PhD, ACSW, LCSW, is Assistant Professor at the School of Social Work at Loyola University in Chicago and maintains a private practice. His work focuses on family therapy and the training and supervision of clinical social workers. His research and practice interests include the use of family therapy to treat severe mental illness, the subjective experience of the mentally ill, and the effect of social-environmental factors on the severely mentally ill. Dr. Marley's writings have appeared in *Social Work,* the *American Journal of Orthopsychiatry,* and the *Journal of Family Psychotherapy.*

CONTENTS

Preface

The focus of this book is on the involvement of families in the treatment of schizophrenia. With that single focus in mind, this book attempts to help students and clinicians better understand the models available for working with families, how each model can be applied to the clinical process of working with families, and what the research demonstrates regarding the effectiveness of the models. In addition, a number of professional issues are examined that have direct impact on the provision of family services for this population.

Working with individuals who have schizophrenia from a family orientation can be difficult. With the emphasis on psychopharmacological interventions, brief hospitalizations, and short-term therapy, many clinicians simply do not see a role for the family in the treatment of the illness. Many families, once pathologized and blamed for the presence of schizophrenia in their household, are now marginalized or forgotten in the treatment process. This trend is in spite of abundant research that indicates family involvement has a critical role to play in the long-term stability of a person with schizophrenia (Dixon and Lehman, 1995).

Why this trend away from family involvement in treating schizophrenia? First, the continued stigma associated with the illness makes many families reluctant to get involved. Many tell me they expect to be blamed for the illness, and that bad parenting is the cause, despite advances in our understanding of the root causes of schizophrenia. Second, family therapists get referrals for families struggling with a "severe and chronic mental illness" and do not see that they have much to offer. Third, family therapists are often constrained by managed care contracts and the limits placed on number of sessions. Finally, many families, tired and burned out from trying to cope with such an illness, give up their involvement. Into this vacuum come case managers, paraprofessionals, and others who may not be educated about or trained in family involvement or who are not very knowledgeable about schizophrenia.

In many ways, the field of family therapy got its start by working with the illness of schizophrenia. Freud, Harry Stack Sullivan, and

Frieda Fromm-Reichmann all hypothesized about the role of the family in the development and presentation of schizophrenia in some of their patients. However, none of them formally chose to work with the family in question. It was not until the 1940s and 1950s when the groundbreaking work of Gregory Bateson and others in Palo Alto, California, brought the notions of family systems and family dynamics directly to their clinical research on schizophrenia. Bateson, along with Jay Haley, Don Jackson, and John Weakland developed some of the foundational concepts on the role of the family in understanding schizophrenia. Their work led to increased interest in observing family interactions when schizophrenia is present.

Somewhat concurrently with this work at Palo Alto was the work of Theodore Lidz and Lyman Wynne. Lidz, although trained in traditional psychoanalytic theory and technique, broke away from some of the traditional dogma and explored the role of fathers and patterns in marital relationships that might have some bearing on schizophrenia. He rejected Fromm-Reichmann's notion that maternal rejection caused schizophrenia. Wynne worked at the National Institute of Mental Health for several decades where he explored the issues of family communication and family roles in better understanding schizophrenia. He was noted for his research expertise, a rigorous examination of family concepts, and their application to schizophrenia that had been missing from some of the literature. Many of these clinicians and researchers were instrumental in training the next generation of family therapists who developed some of the models discussed in this book. Unfortunately, as the second and third generations of family therapists began to practice and expand many of these models of family therapy, they moved further and further away from working with schizophrenia.

I have had the opportunity to work with people with schizophrenia for the past twenty years, fifteen of those as primarily a family therapist. Although this book is not about how I go about my work, it is possible that my biases will show through here and there. My primary bias is the belief that family involvement is critical to the treatment of schizophrenia. My concern has been the withdrawal of family therapists from their active role in the treatment of schizophrenia. The combination of my bias and concern motivated the writing of this book. It is not my intent to convince the reader that one model is superior to all other models. The reader will have to draw his or her own conclusions based on the strengths and weaknesses of each model presented. This book is not meant to be an exhaustive discussion of each model, only a starting point for those interested in the involvement of families in the treatment of schizophrenia.

In this book, I hope to strengthen what has become a weak relationship. Those clinicians and students primarily focused on family intervention and those who are interested primarily in helping families cope with the devastation of schizophrenia will find common ground in this book. Reuniting these two forces can bring about high-quality services to these families by clinicians and students who see family involvement as not only relevant but crucial to the treatment of schizophrenia.

Acknowledgments

I would like to acknowledge several people in my life who have helped shape this book. Judy Nelsen and Wynne Korr have served as mentors for many years covering my graduate and doctoral studies at the University of Illinois at Chicago. My continued involvement with the severely mentally ill is due in large part to the guidance and encouragement offered by these two important individuals. Sant Singh served as my supervisor and family therapy trainer while I was working at the University of Chicago Department of Psychiatry. Any claim I can make to being a good family therapist is due to his careful and patient supervision. To my students, too numerous to mention by name, who sat through my classes at the University of Illinois at Urbana-Champaign and Loyola University Chicago, I give my thanks for making me think out loud about how and why I do the things I do when working with families living with schizophrenia. Your questions and challenges were an important learning tool in my own development.

My thanks to Joe Walsh, Dean of the School of Social Work at Loyola University Chicago, for support that allowed me the opportunity to write this book. Thank you, too, to my colleagues at Loyola who make the environment such a clinically exciting place to teach, study, and write. My thanks also go to the people at The Haworth Press and especially Terry Trepper, for giving me the opportunity to write this book.

Finally, I would like to acknowledge a person who never realized his influence on this project. In the late 1980s I had several opportunities to meet and talk with Carl Whitaker. In those all-too-brief exchanges I found a "kindred spirit" whose work I return to again and again. His style, humor, and intelligence have provided me an endless source of wisdom and encouragement.

Chapter 1

Overview of Schizophrenia

WHAT IS SCHIZOPHRENIA?

Schizophrenia is a form of severe mental illness that affects approximately 1 percent of the population of the world (Robins and Regier, 1991), regardless of gender, age, economic status, or ethnic or racial characteristics. The American Psychiatric Association (2000) defines it as "a disorder that lasts for at least six months and includes at least one month of active-phase symptoms (i.e., two [or more] of the following: delusions, hallucinations, disorganized speech, grossly disorganized or catatonic behavior, negative symptoms)" (p. 298).

The common symptoms of schizophrenia are usually classified as either positive or negative. Positive symptoms are hallucinations and delusions, and negative symptoms include social withdrawal, anhedonia, apathy, and a general inability to interact with others in a socially appropriate way. Cognitive symptoms, which include confused thinking and confused speech, may be a separate category. Individuals with schizophrenia may have some or many of these symptoms. For many, the illness is chronic and severe and they will experience these frightening symptoms periodically for most of their lives. It is not surprising, then, to discover that the suicide rate for people with schizophrenia is higher than among those who suffer from other types of mental illness. Schizophrenia is considered by many mental health professionals to be one of the most disabling mental illnesses (Grinspoon, 1998).

The average age of onset for schizophrenia is the late teens through young adult years. Although rare, it is possible to find children and younger adolescents with this diagnosis. It is even rarer for someone in middle-to-late adulthood to suddenly develop the full syndrome of schizophrenia. Women may be more prone than men for late-onset schizophrenia. Such occurrences have raised concerns about changes in women's physiological functioning following menopause. Research data suggest men develop the disorder earlier in life and may develop a more severe type of schizophrenia. This illness is believed to run in families. Studies examining the rates of occurrence in identical twins versus fraternal twins show a higher incidence among identical twins. However, the concurrence is not exact and lends support to the idea that other factors, besides strict genetic inheritance, play a part in developing the disorder.

In general, schizophrenia can follow a number of courses, depending on the age of onset, severity of the illness, and treatment received. The original term used to define schizophrenia, *dementia praecox,* implies a chronic and deteriorating course for the ill individual, something akin to Alzheimer's disease. Some who develop schizophrenia experience such a course regardless of treatment received. Others, however, may experience a significant decline in functioning during the active phase of the illness, and then the recovery of some or most of their functioning once they receive adequate treatment. These individuals may experience some residual loss of functioning and require ongoing support and services to help them adapt to life following active occurrences of the illness. Still others may experience a sudden onset of acute schizophrenia, receive adequate treatment, and return to their full level of functioning. These individuals may be prone to future bouts of the illness, but can function very well. The variety of courses and symptoms schizophrenia can take has led to the theory that it may actually be a series of related syndromes as opposed to a single disease.

WHAT CAUSES SCHIZOPHRENIA?

Schizophrenia, or the schizophrenia syndrome, is conceptualized as a neurological illness (or related illnesses) whose etiology resides in some still unspecified genetic or physiological anomaly that leads to its characteristic symptoms. Much of the research on the etiology of schizophrenia has focused on the structure and functioning of specific parts of the brain.

The structure of the brain can be analyzed through the use of computed tomography (CT) scans and magnetic resonance imaging (MRI). Research on the structure of brains in people with schizophrenia has not identified anything specific to the disorder but has identified several anomalies (Miller, 2001). In general, individuals with schizophrenia have larger brain ventricles. Ventricles are cavities in the brain filled with spinal fluid. Also, the average size of the brains of people with schizophrenia is somewhat smaller than the average person. Areas that have been found to be smaller include the cerebral cortex, temporal lobes, and the limbic region. Some of the brain's functioning can be analyzed using positron emission tomography (PET) and functional MRI. Some of the research conducted on people with schizophrenia has indicated problematic blood flow to the prefrontal cortex of the brain (Miller, 2001), the area of the brain associated with planning, judgment, and decision making.

Two chemicals in the brain have also been studied to better understand the etiology of schizophrenia. Dopamine and glutamate are neurotransmitters that pass signals between nerve cells. Dopamine has been studied for many years and many of the antipsychotic medications used in treating schizophrenia try to affect the amount of dopamine in the brain. Glutamate is a chemical produced in the cerebral cortex and is necessary in the management of communication between the cortex and other regions of the brain. Changes in the production and transmission of these chemicals indicate they are probably involved in the development of schizophrenia.

Miller (2001) sums up the current view of the etiology of schizophrenia:

> The picture . . . that emerges is a disturbance of processing and coordination in circuits that connect the cerebral cortex and the limbic system, with some involvement of the cerebellum and thalamus. Mutual responsiveness in these pathways is inadequate, communications are mistimed, and associations are misplaced. It becomes difficult to monitor correct language, thought, and behavior; to distinguish external from internal stimuli and significant from trivial information. (pp. 2-3)

Miller indicates much is still unknown about the etiology of schizophrenia. The interactions between genes, neurochemical processes, and the environment are very complex and in need of extensive further study.

HOW IS SCHIZOPHRENIA DIAGNOSED?

The American Psychiatric Association (2000) outlines the salient features required to make the diagnosis of schizophrenia. Included in the diagnosis are

1. the characteristic symptoms of schizophrenia (delusions, hallucinations, disorganized speech, disorganized or catatonic behavior, and negative symptoms);
2. the presence of social/occupational dysfunction;
3. duration of symptoms for at least six months;
4. the ability to exclude the diagnoses of schizoaffective disorder and mood disorder; and
5. the ability to exclude the influence of a substance or medical condition as the cause of the symptoms.

The five subtypes of schizophrenia are: (1) paranoid type, (2) disorganized type, (3) catatonic type, (4) undifferentiated type, and (5) residual type. Each subtype is differentiated by the predominant symptoms present at the time of the evaluation.

Several tools are available to the clinician to aid in the accurate diagnosis of schizophrenia. The Structured Clinical Interview for the DSM-IV Axis-I Disorders, Clinical Version (SCID-I), is a structured interview schedule (First et al., 1997). The structured interview allows a clinician to walk through a specific interview schedule and obtain information relevant to the presence or absence of the diagnostic behaviors and thoughts indicative of the illness. Training is required to be able to appropriately use SCID-I in either a clinical or research setting. Another tool available is the Brief Psychiatric Rating Scale (Lukoff, Nuechterlein, and Ventura, 1986). Developed through research on people with schizophrenia, it allows a trained clinician to obtain information about the presence and severity of specific behaviors and thoughts related to the diagnosis of schizophrenia. Although not as structured as the SCID-I, it can be a useful tool for clinicians who need a format to more readily identify those individuals who may have schizophrenia or some form of psychosis.

THE IMPACT OF SCHIZOPHRENIA

The impact of schizophrenia can be considered from several different points: personal, social, and economic. Each point focuses on a different aspect of the illness and indicates the far-reaching effect this illness has on families, mental health professionals, and society as a whole.

The personal impact of schizophrenia is the greatest. Each day thousands of families must contend with the stress and strain associated with caring for someone with schizophrenia. Likewise, these ill individuals must contend with the social isolation, disrupted life development, and fear and anxiety brought on by the troubling symptoms and their aftermath. The influence and power of stigma, both for individuals with the illness and their families, can lead them to experience a powerlessness and isolation that directly affects their ability to cope with the illness. Families can experience grief, guilt, anger, humiliation, fear, and anxiety over the illness and over ill family members.

The social impact of schizophrenia can best be seen by the prevalence of homelessness and its associated problems in many communities around the country. Torrey (1997) indicates that, based on several large research studies, the number of homeless individuals in the United States was approximately 125,000 in 1980 and 402,000 in 1988. More recent estimates from the Urban Institute (2000) indicate approximately 3.5 million people will likely experience homelessness in a given year. This is a 300 percent increase over a span of eight years. The total population of the United States only increased 7.6 percent during the same time frame. A number of studies (e.g., Goering et al., 2002; Lehman and Cordray, 1993) indicate that nearly 75 percent of homeless individuals are mentally ill, and approximately 35 percent could be considered severely mentally ill. Many homeless individuals engage in illegal activity to obtain money for food, drugs, shelter, and clothing. Although the homeless mentally ill may commit crimes against other people, they are also prone to be victimized by others. Marley and Buila (1999, 2001) found people with severe mental illness to have much higher rates of victimization than the general population.

The economic impact of schizophrenia is often little appreciated by many mental health professionals and the general public. The major costs of schizophrenia can be figured from two perspectives: (1) the cost in dollars to care for these ill individuals, and (2) the cost in dollars of lost employment and productivity brought on by this devastating illness. The first cost has been well documented. In the United States, approximately one million people suffer from schizophrenia (about 1 percent of the population [Robins and Regier, 1991]). Yet these individuals account for approximately 75 percent of the total mental health services expenditures. Weiden and Olfson (1995) found the cost for inpatient treatment for people with schizophrenia in the United States in 1986 was about 2.3 billion dollars. The cost for readmission following relapse was about 2 billion dollars. Due to the chronic and severe nature of the illness, many individuals rely on public aid or other government assistance to pay for their frequent hospitalizations and outpatient services. Many of these government assistance programs do not cover the true cost of providing intensive, high quality, long-term care for people with severe schizophrenia. As a result, many of these individuals receive inadequate care. In some cases, the families of people with schizophrenia must pay out of pocket for adequate care. This puts an additional burden on families whose coping skills are already stretched thin by trying to manage the day-to-day reality of caring for someone with schizophrenia.

Chapter 2

Families and Schizophrenia

HISTORICAL RELATIONSHIP BETWEEN THE ILLNESS AND THE FAMILY

The relationship between schizophrenia and the family has been long and contentious. Over the course of the past century in particular, families have had to endure numerous theories that have labeled them the cause of the illness. This was not always the case, and the emergence of such theories speaks to the growing frustration professionals face in understanding the illness and the need to exert power on the often-powerless families devastated by the illness.

In its original, or at least early, conceptualization, schizophrenia was understood as a biological illness. No mention was made of the family or its possible role in the development or course of the illness. In fact, throughout the eighteenth and nineteenth centuries, the focus of treatment for the bizarre symptoms of the illness (the term "schizophrenia" did not emerge until the twentieth century) was on the individual.

With the advent of psychoanalysis in the early twentieth century, and its adoption by American medical professionals, the focus shifted to early life events and the role of family on the development of psychopathology. Family, however, was essentially narrowed down to mean the mother and the mothering the ill individual received. As schizophrenia was considered a sign of severe regression to infantile or pre-oedipal functioning, the traumatic experiences thought to cause schizophrenia were believed to have happened in the earliest stages of life. Because mothers were considered the primary caregivers, failure to develop normally was seen as indicative of poor mothering. The term "schizophrenigenic mother," coined by Frieda Fromm-Reichmann, has, unfortunately, continued to be an underlying assumption still found among some mental health professionals. The term implied that a particular type of mothering was the cause of schizophrenia. Although psychoanalysis continued to hold sway over the field through the 1950s, a new line of research raised some concerns about the relevance of psychoanalysis in understanding the etiology of schizophrenia.

The advent of medication to treat schizophrenia began somewhat by accident in the 1950s. These early medications were primarily considered major tranquilizers and simply sedated the individual with schizophrenia, thus making him or her easier to manage. As new medications were developed, more practitioners were again asking if schizophrenia really had its etiological roots in some biological process. Throughout the 1970s and up until the present, more research has focused on identifying the neurobiological roots of schizophrenia.

However, the strength of psychoanalysis and related theories caused some continued family or parental blame to persist even in the face of new neurological research. The ability of psychoanalysis to provide a theory for the etiology of schizophrenia seems minimal, and its ability to provide a theory for treating schizophrenia continues to be a controversial topic. The confusion between a theory of etiology and a theory of treatment still remains. As a consequence, even though most mental health professionals understand schizophrenia to be a neurophysiological illness, family or parental blame still persists. Although the influence of psychoanalysis has waned, especially as it relates to schizophrenia, many family members still report that they are made to feel guilty about the presence of schizophrenia in their families.

The conceptualization of schizophrenia and the role of the family have gone full circle. What was once perceived to be a biological illness is again primarily seen in that light. The role of the family, once ignored completely, is again minimized in the face of mounting biological research and a focus on psychotropic medication as the treatment of choice. Despite this cyclical history, family members continue to provide the majority of care for individuals with schizophrenia and continue to try and cope with the confusing and devastating effects of the illness (Marley, 1992).

IMPACT OF SCHIZOPHRENIA ON THE FAMILY

One framework for understanding the impact of schizophrenia on the family is the family developmental life cycle (McGoldrick, Heiman, and Carter, 1993). This model incorporates key principles and second order changes across the life span of the family and its members. Although the model assumes biological/marital relatedness in defining family, all family types can experience some of the issues raised. For the purpose of this discussion the person with schizophrenia will be viewed as the biological offspring of a married couple.

The Young Couple

Concerns about mental illness can begin before the presence of children. Genetics and the focus of biological psychiatry have heightened public awareness of how some illnesses are transmitted. Unfortunately, the issue of "family blame" for perpetuating a mental illness can be one result of faulty biological reasoning. Newly married couples may consciously or unconsciously react to a family history of mental illness. The presence of a relative with schizophrenia or some other severe mental illness can increase anxiety about having children.

Mental health professionals must be aware of this potential source of stress. One intervention is to help sort fact from fiction. All families have their own mythology and reasoning for explaining some historic odd behavior or abnormality. Careful questioning on the part of the mental health professional about the family history as well as careful investigation by the couple can alleviate some of this anxiety. Mental health professionals must be well educated about the genetics and biology of severe mental illness to better inform these couples.

Families with Young Children

With the birth of children, the family undergoes a restructuring process. A couple must adapt to the presence of others in the system. This process affects not only the child but also grandparents and other relatives. Parenting roles are developed as well as changes in the division of labor. The child also undergoes tremendous change during the first six years of his or her life. The psychological, cognitive, and social development sets the foundation that carries the person into adolescence and adulthood.

Research is exploring the early detection of possible serious mental illness in children (Grinspoon, 1995). The research indicates there may be subtle changes in the behavior of children that are related to the onset of schizophrenia. Whether the child is clumsy, isolative, or delayed in reaching maturational milestones, mental illness may begin to take its toll at an early age. There are several positive ramifications of this line of research. First, early detection may lead to more successful early intervention. Second, parents could receive services to help them adapt to unexpected parental roles and develop the necessary skills to help cope with a possible lifelong illness. Third, the larger family system should be assessed. The roles played by grandparents and other relatives have a long tradition of importance in many cultures. Also, siblings of troubled children must be provided services to help them cope with the stress, embarrassment, and confusion they may feel.

Families with Adolescents

Adolescents introduce many changes into the family system. The role of parent undergoes change to allow for the increasing independence and unique identity of the adolescent. Parents may begin to look at midlife marital and career issues. Adolescents undergo several changes as well. The onset of puberty, sexual maturation, self-identity development, concrete and formal operational thinking, and changes in peer group relations result in dramatic changes in their lifestyle and understanding of the world. Even in healthy families, this can be a stressful time.

Research shows that schizophrenia primarily manifests itself during adolescence (American Psychiatric Association, 2000; Gerhart, 1990). The onset of schizophrenia in an adolescent has many consequences for the family. First, there is the unanticipated stress on the family system that includes parents, siblings, grandparents, and other relatives. Second, the process of adapting family boundaries may be a confusing experience. The adolescent with schizophrenia may not be able to move in and out of the family system in a healthy and appropriate way. Such movement occurs in the process of increasing independence. Yet the family may be confused about the level of appropriateness of independence for the adolescent. Such confusion can result in rigid and overprotective boundaries. Third, the presence of the illness results in a constant focus on the illness. The concerns of the parents about midlife marital and career issues get put on hold. The couple must rethink and adjust to new priorities. They may become hostile toward their adolescent with schizophrenia as they feel their lives and aspirations must be set aside to cope with the illness. Guilt and shame about their feelings of hostility may follow. Finally, the adolescent with schizophrenia may be unable to form friendships or utilize a peer group. Such interpersonal deficits can limit social and support networks later in life.

Launching Children and Moving On

Family at this stage is characterized by the return to the marital couple, an important step in the development of a marriage. As children move on, parents can focus on their marriage, careers, and address concerns of supporting and caring for their own parents. Parents and children form adult-adult relationships. Children focus on separation from parents and the family system through school, work, and relationships. This move into society as an independent adult is key to managing later-life issues.

The presence of a young adult with schizophrenia in the family is felt most strongly at this stage. Attachment to school, work, or relationships may not be possible. Difficulty forming friendships and peer groups limits their social options and support. The illness may have made school an unsuccessful experience and the formation of a cohesive sense of self a confusing experience. The process of launching from the family is a stressful and, at times, impossible task.

Failure to return to the original marital couple can place stress on the parents. Marital friction can be directed toward and blamed on the young adult with schizophrenia. Parents may also be confused about their responsibility to the young adult. They may wonder if they should make the young adult move out of the house and into a treatment program, but then be unclear as to what their options are and if such a move will make them appear selfish. They may wonder how to control a young adult with schizophrenia in their house and how to set appropriate boundaries and respond to troubling symptoms and behaviors. Tremendous strain is put on the couple both as individuals and as partners in a marriage.

The Family in Later Life

There are several dynamics at play in families at this stage. As the parents get older, they focus on their own health and well-being.

Family roles change as the children become parents and the parents become grandparents. Loss of a spouse or other family members occurs. The older generation can be utilized for their experience and wisdom. The younger generation adapts to caring for and supporting the older generation.

The primary stress facing a family with an adult child with schizophrenia is the concern over the future. "What will happen to my child after I die?" "Who will be responsible for ensuring appropriate care, housing, and financial support?" These questions often come up when the family is in crisis following the death of a family member. It is difficult to plan for meaningful support and long-term goals in the midst of a crisis. These fears are not unique to the parents and relatives. The adult with schizophrenia, too, has these fears. This is particularly true of more seriously impaired individuals who require long-term care and support. Relatives often will be reluctant to take over primary care from the parents. With a lack of concrete information on how the problem will be dealt with, the adult with schizophrenia may invent facts or a solution that is often more frightening than reality. Such invented facts can include the fear that he or she will end up living on the streets or that he or she may have no money, no family support, or no social support.

FAMILY ISSUES WHEN CONFRONTED WITH SCHIZOPHRENIA

The use of the family developmental life cycle brings to the surface a number of key issues families confront when living with, caring for, or supporting a family member with schizophrenia.

Financial Planning and Education

Knowledge of funding sources available to help families cope at all stages of development is integral to successful management of the illness. Many families see the current system of funding bodies as confusing, disjointed, and overwhelming. Families will require education and support to better access the options available to them. Clinicians working with these families must also be educated about the options available for financial assistance. Reliance only on Medicaid and disability insurance, although important, can be limiting for the family. Other areas such as a trust fund, estate planning, and private insurance can be evaluated and utilized. The National Alliance for the Mentally Ill (see Chapter 14) has taken some leadership in developing educational material about this topic.

Long-Term Access to Consumer Support Groups

Parents, siblings, grandparents, relatives, and the individual with schizophrenia need access to support groups, which can be important resources for developing social and support networks. Many consumer/family support groups provide educational material, workshops, publications, and meetings that can help alleviate some of the anxiety, anger, frustration, isolation, and embarrassment experienced by the family.

Family-Oriented Services That Can Change over Time

The family developmental life cycle has its drawbacks, but the model identifies the needs experienced by families at different stages of their development. Likewise, the services available to families must change along with the family. A family with an adolescent with schizophrenia needs different services than a family coping with an older adult with schizophrenia. The extent to which mental health professionals can be attentive to these developmental shifts will help the family get what it needs from such professionals. Since schizophrenia affects families of all types, it will be important to explore the intersection of family development and schizophrenia as experienced by families of color, single-parent families, adoptive families, remarried families, and gay and lesbian families.

A Long-Term Frame of Mind

Many traditional models of family intervention in treating schizophrenia do not take the life-span view of the illness or the family. Clinicians who work with this population from a family perspective need to adopt a long-term frame of mind to better understand and anticipate some of what a family needs or wants in order to move through life with decreased conflict and increased adaptation. Clinicians may have to function as educators, therapists, case managers, and motivators.

What do families who are coping with schizophrenia want from mental health professionals? Although each family has its own unique needs, there are some general expectations that arise from their feedback. These families would like respect; accurate information about the illness, its etiology, course, and treatment; interventions that are sensitive to the needs of the whole family; and interventions that do not perpetuate blame or guilt about the illness.

The following chapters outline what some of these interventions are and how they might work in providing services to these families. Each intervention has its own strengths and weaknesses. Mental health professionals will have to judge for themselves the merits of each and select the ones that are most applicable to their work setting, target population, and own unique style.

Chapter 3

Psychodynamic Family Therapy

BRIEF OVERVIEW AND APPLICATION TO SCHIZOPHRENIA

Early Pioneers

Given the role psychoanalytic theory has played in our understanding of schizophrenia, it is no surprise that some of the early pioneers in the development of family therapy were trained in and worked with these individuals from this theoretical perspective. Such pioneers included Theodore Lidz, Nathan Ackerman, James Framo, Ivan Boszormenyi-Nagy, Lyman Wynne, Carl Whitaker, Don Jackson, Salvador Minuchin, and Murray Bowen. Some retained a decidedly psychoanalytic flavor to their family therapy work, and others moved further and further away from strict adherence to psychoanalytic concepts. A few others rejected outright the theory of psychoanalysis.

Psychoanalysis as a theory of human development, pathology, and treatment provided a wealth of ideas that could be incorporated into working with families. Nathan Ackerman and Ivan Boszormenyi-Nagy created centers for the study of families and were influential in training other family therapists in the use of psychoanalytic theory. When the National Institute of Mental Health (NIMH) opened in the early 1950s it attracted Lyman Wynne, who was particularly interested in studying families of individuals with schizophrenia.

In 1965, Ivan Boszormenyi-Nagy and James Framo collaborated as editors and produced the highly influential *Intensive Family Therapy: Theoretical and Practical Aspects*. This book included foundational work related to family therapy with schizophrenia by Murray Bowen, Nathan Ackerman, Lyman Wynne, Carl Whitaker, and Harold Searles. Other authors (e.g., Robbins, 1993) have advocated for the use of psychoanalysis in the treatment of schizophrenia. However, some of them propose an individual approach to treating the illness.

As psychoanalysis has developed over the years, several theoretical schools have emerged that use it as their basis. Object-relations theory, self-psychology, and ego psychology each build on certain key elements of traditional psychoanalytic theory.

Although it is beyond the scope of this text to give a thorough review of the theory of psychoanalysis, there are several key concepts that seem relevant to family work with schizophrenia. The focus of this discussion will be on the work of family therapists who treat families coping with schizophrenia from a psychoanalytic orientation. The work of Murray Bowen and Carl Whitaker, who operated from this perspective, will be addressed in later chapters.

Lyman Wynne

Lyman Wynne and his colleagues at the NIMH developed two important ideas from their work with families. *Pseudomutuality* is a false presentation of togetherness that prevents the actual family conflict from being observed (Wynne et al., 1958). *Pseudohostility* is a superficial experience, one that supposedly demonstrates family conflict but actually misdirects therapists away from the source of the real conflict and minimizes the degree of the conflict (Wynne, 1961). These two family dynamics form a kind of defense mechanism that prevents therapists from seeing underlying conflict and allows families to maintain a rigid control over how they are perceived by outsiders.

Wynne (1965), in discussing his ideas about exploratory family therapy, outlines a number of concepts arising out of work with schizophrenia. Trading of dissociations "means that each person deals most focally with that in the other which the other cannot acknowledge. Thus, there can be no meeting, no confirmation, no mutality, no shared validation of feelings or experience" (p. 299). Wynne views this concept as related to the psychoanalytic concept of projective identification. Collective cognitive chaos is experienced as a family-level phenomena in which the transactional and communicative patterns are blatantly bizarre and fractured. Fixed distancing was experienced as a kind of rigid boundary and emotional cutoff from each family member. In the face of bizarre or chaotic behavior, some family members act in a rigid and detached manner as if they are oblivious to the troubling behavior. A final concept derived from Wynne's work is the notion of amorphous communication. Such communication is defined by its vague and undirected nature. It often leaves family and individual expectations unclear.

Ivan Boszormenyi-Nagy

Ivan Boszormenyi-Nagy (1965) developed a number of concepts closely tied to traditional psychoanalytic theory. His model of intensive family therapy "requires all family members to open up long-aching personal wounds in an atmosphere of mutually, though reluctantly, rescinded privacy" (p. 97). Phenomena such as acting out, family patterns, and other defense mechanisms prevent individuation on the part of family members and thus prevent the kind of opening up and insight hoped for by the model.

Nathan Ackerman and Paul Franklin

Nathan Ackerman and Paul Franklin (1965) discuss the role of schizophrenia in the context of homeostatic disorder and imbalance in the family. Their goal is to readjust the family's homeostatic equilibrium and thereby adjust the course and behavior of the person with schizophrenia. They believe that the family and the person with schizophrenia were locked in a circular process, each affecting the other in an attempt to establish some kind of balance within the family. Balance is achieved at a potentially high cost to the ill individual. Scapegoating and dependency attachments, for example, may be ways the family achieves such balance.

James Framo

James Framo, who functioned somewhat independently from the major family therapy models, incorporated psychoanalytic concepts into his family therapy with schizophrenia. Framo (1965) wrote extensively about the idea of resistance to change in family therapy. He believes "Families, too, conceive of change in terms of deprivation rather than enhancement, and, at the deepest level, they fear change in the family system which will result in loss of some vitally needed form of relationship, even if the relationship has its hurting aspects"

(p. 181). Family dynamics, communication patterns, acting out, scapegoating, and other phenomena may indicate the family's basic fear of change and the struggle to maintain some form of balance even if it hurts one of the family members.

Although there are numerous other core concepts derived from psychoanalysis and its related theories, the techniques used in psychoanalytic family therapy are relatively straightforward. Several of the most pertinent ones and their application to working with schizophrenia are discussed in the following text.

ESSENTIAL SKILLS AND TECHNIQUES

Nichols and Schwartz (2001) define the goal of psychoanalytic family therapy as "to free family members of unconscious restrictions so that they'll be able to interact with one another as a whole, healthy person" (p. 213). The skills and techniques of psychoanalytic family therapy should be the means to reach this end. At a basic level, the two most essential skills are listening and interpretation.

Psychoanalytical Listening

Psychoanalytical listening involves both auditory and visual observing (Langs, 1973). The therapist must listen for the messages conveyed by the client at both direct and indirect levels. Direct levels are the overt messages and information being shared by the client. Indirect levels are the covert messages that may require interpretation or inference to decode their meaning. The therapist must also attend to the metacommunication occurring in the encounter. Metacommunication emerges out of the unique mix of overt messages, covert messages, and the emerging interactional relationship between the therapist and client. Within the process of family therapy, direct and indirect messages exist at both an individual and a family level. What is being said helps develop the content of the family therapy. How it is being said and for what purpose helps develop the context of the family therapy (Marley, 1992). When working with families trying to cope with schizophrenia, the issue of listening takes on additional complexity. The family as a whole and the therapist must struggle to understand the communication of the person with schizophrenia and how such potentially disordered communication interacts with the family's overall communication style.

Interpretation

Interpretation is a standard technique in most psychoanalytical therapy. It relies on the ability of the therapist to draw inferences from the statements made by the clients. Interpretation is defined as a "Procedure which, by means of analytic investigation, brings out the latent meaning in what the subject says and does. Interpretation reveals the modes of the defensive conflict and its ultimate aim is to identify the wish that is expressed by every product of the unconscious" (Laplanche and Pontalis, 1973, p. 227).

The notion that the communications of people with schizophrenia can have latent and manifest meanings and be used as a form of defense against psychological injury has been well discussed in the literature. Studies by Forrest (1976), Lanin-Kettering and Harrow (1985), and Rutter (1985) have all addressed the clinical relevance of trying to understand the latent and manifest statements of people with schizophrenia. The role of the family therapist becomes one of trying to help the family listen and interpret what the relative with schizophrenia is trying to communicate (Marley, 1992). Such empathic attunement can help decrease the level of anxiety experienced by both the family and the relative with schizophrenia, anxiety often generated by miscommunication and misunderstanding. With the increased focus on the neurobiology of schizophrenia, the focus has moved away from seeing the disordered or idiosyncratic speech of people with schizophrenia as an indicator of a psychological defense mechanism and toward the notion that it is an outcome of some neurobiological process. Interpreting the speech of people with schizophrenia, therefore, is currently a controversial topic.

One area that is less controversial is the use of interpretation to point out family resistance. Many families engage in conscious or unconscious resistance to change. In families where schizophrenia is present, some prefer the status quo even if it means one individual is the scapegoat. As I have explained it to my family therapy students, some families do not like what they have, but at least they know what it is. Some types of resistance that need to be pointed out through interpretation may be the continued blaming of the ill individual for all of the family's problems, an inability to answer questions about family history, a reluctance to follow through with specific homework assignments, or missing or being late to family therapy appointments.

Therapist Neutrality

Therapist neutrality is another technique used in psychoanalytic family therapy. Neutrality is an attitude the therapist develops that prevents him or her from acting on or directing the therapy according to some ideal plan based on assumptions due to values or theoretical beliefs (Laplanche and Pontalis, 1973). In its extreme, many see this as a kind of robotic, unresponsive, unfeeling therapist who rarely speaks and gives no indication of how he or she is thinking about the family. This was certainly not the intent of the concept. Rather, it is the belief that the therapist must be careful not to form hasty judgments based on preconceived notions that arise from either aspects of the family (such as ethnic or cultural assumptions) or from the theory of psychoanalysis (such as hearing only what is supported by the theory and disregarding the rest).

In family therapy with people coping with schizophrenia, such neutrality is important. As mentioned earlier, some early formulations of the cause of schizophrenia blamed the maternal caregiving received during infancy. Although such notions are not supported by the research on the etiology of schizophrenia, family and parental blame can still be implied or assumed by some clinicians who take a hostile attitude toward caregivers. The hostile attitude can lead parents or caregivers to second guess their motives and decisions, often making them feel guilty about their caregiving and angry with the clinician. Neutrality has been criticized by many postmodern theorists who see it as an unobtainable (and unwarranted) therapeutic concept. They argue that every clinician brings to the therapeutic encounter a host of biases that will play out in the therapeutic process. Many traditional psychoanalytic therapists have turned their attention to this idea and have reconsidered the concept of neutrality. Some now see the client-therapist interaction as a mutually constructed experience that is built around the biases and histories of each participant and their interaction.

THE PROCESS OF FAMILY THERAPY

How then does the psychoanalytic family therapy with schizophrenia proceed? In most cases, the therapy takes on a nondirective and exploratory process in which the family therapist asks questions and probes for material that will illuminate the psychological functioning of each individual and of the family as a whole. It is less about specific techniques than about careful questioning, the use of interpretation, and listening at multiple levels for the meaning of communication from each person and from the family as a whole.

Joining

Psychoanalytic family therapy with schizophrenia is often a long-term process that involves the entire family. The therapist's first task is to join with the family. Such joining allows the therapist to see how the family functions from the inside and to better gather information about the family's psychological functioning. Harry Stack Sullivan (1974) and Nathan Ackerman (1961) both advocated for this intimate type of connection between clinician and the family (in Ackerman's case) or the person with schizophrenia (in Sullivan's case). By personally connecting to each family member, through expressions of concern, by probing questions, and through occasional provocative statements, the therapist forms an alliance with the family.

Alliances

The formation of the alliance allows for, or sets the emotional stage for, the opening up and honest exploration of the family members' emotional and psychological life. Ackerman (1961), Whitaker, Felder, and Warkentin (1965), and Framo (1992) indicate that at times, the therapist must use self-revealing as a technique to further this process. By identifying personal experiences or reactions to the family members' comments, the therapist can model the kind of emotional expressiveness the family can move toward. Both Whitaker and Ackerman were noted for their sometimes provocative and confrontational manner in family therapy. By saying absurd or emotionally provocative things, both therapists hoped to free up the emotional communication in the family.

Developing an alliance and freeing up communication helps the family begin to deal with its resistances or defenses. The resistance may be toward change in general, toward some change in attitude or behavior, or toward adaptation to a challenging experience such as schizophrenia. In family therapy with schizophrenia, some of the resistance may be to honestly address the emotions created by the presence of schizophrenia. Some members of the family may feel angry toward the person with schizophrenia, but then feel very guilty at feeling angry. Some members may be grieving the loss of the person they once knew or the loss of a future they hoped for. Such strong emotions, often defended against, can lead to problematic behaviors in the family. Arguments, blaming, focusing on work rather than the family, withdrawing from family interactions, developing a detached attitude toward family members, can all indicate some type of hidden emotion that the person is trying to defend against coming to the surface. In many cases, the psychoanalytic family therapy treatment of schizophrenia is focused on bringing these emotions to the surface by interpreting them as defenses and exploring the rationale behind their formation. Often, once such defenses are named and explored in the family therapy setting, changes in attitudes, emotional connectedness, and behaviors toward one another will also change.

Level of Success

Can the person with schizophrenia actively participate in such an insight-oriented process as psychoanalytic family therapy? The historical literature seems to indicate yes. Robbins (1993), from an individual therapy orientation, also indicates the answer is yes. But Robbins raises an interesting paradox when he notes that when a person with schizophrenia benefits from psychoanalytic therapy, many professionals skeptical of psychoanalysis will raise doubts that the person actually has schizophrenia. It seems the bias is toward believing that people with schizophrenia do not have the capacity for insight-oriented treatment. Amador and David (1998) indicate poor insight or lack of insight is a common problem in people suffering from some kind of psychosis. Gabbard (1994) indicates that with careful usage and modification, people with schizophrenia can benefit from psychotherapy. The authors are silent on the issue of psychoanalytic family therapy.

Conclusion

What is the role of psychoanalytic family therapy in the treatment of schizophrenia? The answer is probably "minimal." Fewer clinicians are trained in this orientation, and fewer still work with people with schizophrenia. It may be that the foundational work of the first generation of family therapists must make way for newer models based on newer research into the etiology of the illness. Another reason for the limited role of this model may be the continued confusion between a theory of etiology and a theory of treatment. The extent to which practitioners of psychoanalysis make claims that their theory explains the cause of schizophrenia will continue to marginalize their involvement in treatment. It would be a better use of their time to demonstrate how effective their model is in the family treatment of schizophrenia. Psychoanalysis must also contend with its unfortunate history of parental (read: mother) blame for causing schizophrenia. Such a notion has cast a pall over the model and its relevance to schizophrenia that is still seen to this day. Unfortunately, many concepts developed from this orientation still show some promise in helping families. Careful listening, understanding the manifest and latent aspects of communication, and the attention to the relationship between the therapist and the family are all important tools many clinicians could utilize in their work.

Chapter 4

Bowenian Family Therapy

BRIEF OVERVIEW AND APPLICATION TO SCHIZOPHRENIA

Murray Bowen

The extensive clinical and theoretical work of Murray Bowen provided the foundation for Bowenian family therapy. Bowen, one of the pioneers in family therapy, began his career at the Menninger Clinic and worked there until 1954. From there he went to the National Institute of Mental Health where he was the first director of the Family division. Bowen then went to Georgetown University's Department of Psychiatry in 1959 and remained there for thirty-one years. He died in 1990. Other family therapists who were trained by or have built on Bowen's foundation include Michael Kerr, Daniel Papero, Betty Carter, Thomas Fogarty, Philip Guerin, Peggy Papp, and Monica McGoldrick. James Framo, although not usually associated with Bowen's work, included a number of Bowen's concepts in his work with families. A hallmark of the development and influence of Bowen's work is reflected in *Family Therapy: Theory and Practice* (Guerin, 1976). The book includes important contributions to family work with schizophrenia by Bowen, John Weakland, Carl Whitaker, and C. Christan Beels.

Critical to the early years of Bowen's work and development was his involvement in treating schizophrenia through family therapy. Many of his papers published in the 1950s and 1960s focus on schizophrenia (Bowen, 1978). Out of this work came the formulation of a number of concepts that can be applied to work with families coping with schizophrenia. With, perhaps, the exception of Michael Kerr, most second-generation Bowenian family therapists did little work with schizophrenia. Therefore, to get an overview of Bowen's theory and model, the focus will be on Bowen's own work.

Triangulation

Bowen (1978) felt that the smallest stable system in any family was a triangle, or three-person system. He believed that a two-person system would draw in a third person when under stress or chaos. In a stereotypical arrangement, two parents coping with a young adult with schizophrenia, the parents may pull in the person with schizophrenia as a part of their emotional entanglement. The person with schizophrenia may become the focus of attention to the detriment of the marital relationship. Often this is voiced in family therapy situations such as, "If only our son was fixed we would all be happy" or "We are fine; it's just our son who needs help." In many cases, the third member plays a key role in diffusing the conflict between the parents by providing an easy focus of concern.

Stability is also a relative concept in Bowen's theory. As previously mentioned, stability is often achieved at the cost of another person.

Differentiation

Differentiation of self was, for Bowen (1978), a two-tier phenomenon. One tier focused on the intrapsychic process of differentiating a person's thinking from his or her emotions. The other tier focused on the interpersonal process of differentiating a person's thoughts, feelings, and actions from those of the other members of the family. People who are undifferentiated have difficulty thinking objectively as their emotions are intertwined with their intellect. They may react impulsively and emotionally without thinking through the consequences of their actions. They may be overly reactive to the other family members, often engaging in thoughts or behaviors that seem dictated by the family.

The idea of differentiation in families coping with schizophrenia is somewhat problematic. First, by nature of the illness of schizophrenia, a misconnection often occurs between the person's thoughts and feelings. It is not a function of differentiation but a function of the neurological mechanism of schizophrenia. People with schizophrenia also may be highly reactive to the behaviors of other family members (Marley, 1998), not due to lack of differentiation but as a symptom of their illness. Still, many families coping with schizophrenia, including the person with the illness, have difficulty acting and thinking autonomously. In many cases, the family develops highly rigid and enmeshed boundaries as a defense against or reaction to the chaos brought on by the illness.

For Bowen (1978), the nuclear family's emotional process described the dynamic system of a family. The more undifferentiated a spouse is prior to marriage, the more that anxiety is created once married and there is also a tendency to fuse with the other spouse. Such fusion can lead to marital conflict at a minimum. In extreme cases, such fusion can lead to emotional or physical problems in one of the spouses and the tendency to project onto the children some of the emotional problems of the married couple.

In working with families coping with schizophrenia, it is not uncommon to find the person with schizophrenia at the center of marital problems. Although not etiologically relevant to schizophrenia, marital conflict arising out of problems of differentiation between the spouses can certainly increase the anxiety experienced by the individual with schizophrenia. The emotional environment of the home can be a factor in how the person with schizophrenia copes with the illness. The concept of *expressed emotion* (EE) is common in the literature of the illness as an environmental condition that is related to the relapse of people with schizophrenia (Leff and Vaughn, 1981; Liberman, 1992).

Projection

Projection is the process by which parents transmit their problems onto their child(ren). It is the basic mechanism for achieving the nuclear family's emotional process. Often, it is accomplished through triangulation.

In working with families coping with schizophrenia, it is possible to see this mechanism at work. Subtle signs and symptoms of difficulty may emerge even in childhood. The child may seem more vulnerable or in need of special attention. In some families, one parent may form a very close bond to the vulnerable child, instilling in that child a belief that he or she needs the parent to survive. The parent may get some psychological benefit out of fulfilling this need, feeling special or useful, or alleviating any guilt feelings the parent might have for having a less than perfect child. The other parent, who may have anxiety about the marital relationship and his or her relationship with the child, may foster this attachment to alleviate his or her own level of anxiety. Thus the child serves the parents' needs by being the object on to which the parents project their feelings and concerns. Bowen felt the object of the projection process was likely to be the least differentiated child in the family and mirror the parents' differentiation issues.

The *multigenerational transmission process* (Bowen, 1978) is the playing out of the process of family differentiation and projection across several generations. Bowen felt that some families turn out poorly differentiated children, who go on to marry poorly differentiated spouses, who then turn out even more poorly differentiated children. Bowen hypothesized that if this pattern continued for several generations, it was likely the couple would eventually have a child with schizophrenia. Although research on the etiology of schizophrenia contradicts this notion, the repetition of certain family patterns of emotional and psychological functioning can be seen in many families.

One outcome of the multigenerational transmission process and the continuation of differentiation difficulties can be an emotional cutoff (Bowen, 1978). Some individuals in these types of poorly undifferentiated families may withdraw or cut off contact with their family of origin. Bowen viewed this running away from the problems and the family as a pseudosolution. It looks as though it resolves the problem, but in actuality the person doing the fleeing is still reacting emotionally to the family and acting out his or her own undifferentiated position in the family. Some individuals with schizophrenia may try to run away from or cut off all connections with their families. In some cases, the family may try to sever ties to the person with schizophrenia, often in a last-ditch effort to survive the stress and burden experienced in caring for someone with schizophrenia. The individuals involved usually regret such emotionally charged and impulsive decisions once the initial crisis that spurred the reaction has passed.

ESSENTIAL SKILLS AND TECHNIQUES

The goal of Bowenian family therapy is "to decrease anxiety and increase differentiation of self—nothing else lasts" (Nichols and

Schwartz, 2001, p. 152). From the previous concepts, it is clear Bowen believed people needed to be differentiated on both levels and to use this position to manage their multiple relationships with their family. How then do you achieve this goal with Bowen's theory and model as a guide? Unfortunately, Bowen was not keen on specifying techniques to achieve the goals of his approach to family therapy. Many people who read his work find his theoretical work more sophisticated and developed than most models of family therapy. It is just difficult to figure out what to do to bring these theoretical concepts into the realm of technique and therapeutic action. Many of the second generation Bowenian family therapists have focused their attention on specific techniques.

The Genogram

One of the most important tools to come out of Bowen's theory and model was the development of the genogram. The genogram provides a graphic representation of the multigenerational structure and process of a specific family. The tool of the genogram was best outlined and discussed by McGoldrick and Gerson (1985). Their work details the technique and power of the genogram, both as an assessment tool and as a treatment tool. By graphically depicting the family, both the family and the therapist can map out relationships, dynamics, key historical events, triangles within the family, and the multigenerational nature of the family and its emotional and psychological functioning.

In the treatment of schizophrenia, the genogram can be very helpful. First, it can reinforce the notion of a broader family context and remind the immediate family of potential connections for support. Second, the genogram can demystify some of the historical family issues that may have a direct bearing on the family's attitudes toward the person with schizophrenia. In some cases, families I have worked with have identified other relatives who were eccentric, bizarre, or troubled in some way. Often, these individuals were shrouded in mystery and the family rarely spoke about them. Such secrecy, guilt, shame, or fear based on the family's history can play out in the present when the family is trying to understand why it is difficult to cope with schizophrenia. The genogram can bring these mysteries into the open and prompt important family discussions about biases and beliefs that affect the current family. Many family therapists, including those who do not subscribe to Bowen's theory, make use of the genogram as a fundamental tool for family therapy.

The Process Question

Although Bowen did not specify techniques, he did develop the use of the process question. According to Nichols and Schwartz (2001), such questions "are designed to slow people down, diminish reactive anxiety, and start them thinking—not just about how others are upsetting them, but about how they are involved as participants in interpersonal patterns" (p. 155). The question seeks to not only bring forth new information, but also to show how the person is interacting with the family as a whole. This line of questioning keeps the focus on how a problem or issue affects the entire family. Bowen's concern was modifying the entire family system, not just the individual components.

In working with families coping with schizophrenia, there is often a tendency to focus on the person with schizophrenia and figure out how to fix him or her. It is as though the schizophrenia is a pathogen that must be cut out of the family. Process questions allow the therapist to refocus the discussion on how the family as a whole is affected by the presence of schizophrenia, the reciprocal nature of the family interactions, and how everyone plays a part in establishing the emotional environment within the family.

Detriangling

A final technique, which is more of a process, is detriangling. From Bowen's concept of triangulation and how two people will pull in a third to help alleviate anxiety, detriangling is the process whereby the third person, be it a family member or the therapist, does not become this third person. In many families, when two people have issues with one another, they may try to bring in one other family member or the therapist as a way of not having to confront the issues between them. The therapist may have to actively support the third family member in his or her attempt to not get pulled in to the conflict. Likewise, the therapist will have to carefully observe attempts made by the family to bring the therapist in as the third person.

In family therapy with schizophrenia, often the person with schizophrenia is the third person in the triangle. In a stereotypical example, the parents may focus on the person with schizophrenia in an attempt to not deal directly with each other about marital issues that are sometimes of more immediate importance. The family therapist may need to establish a strong coalition with the person with schizophrenia to give him or her the support needed to step out of the way so that the parents can deal more directly with each other. This coalition building is similar to what structural family therapists do in their sessions.

THE PROCESS OF FAMILY THERAPY

How then does Bowenian family therapy with schizophrenia proceed? Similar to the psychoanalytic process, Bowenian family therapy would be seen as a long-term process that is insight oriented and seeks to increase the level of differentiation within and between each family member. Bowen felt deeply that the clinician had to really understand the idea of the family system, with all of its nuances and complexities. The process of family therapy would naturally emerge out of that understanding. Bowen was less focused on techniques and stages of family therapy, often deriding those who he saw as technicians without theory. Yet in his work with families coping with schizophrenia, some trends or processes come to the surface.

Alliances

First, although Bowen has the reputation of presenting as an aloof theoretician, it is clear he was careful in forming a working alliance with the families. His careful observation and use of process questioning (which in some ways prefigured the idea of circular questioning in the Milan family therapy) allowed him to both uncover family system information and to begin to shift the family into thinking and seeing itself as a system. His work with schizophrenia also demonstrated his sense that the person with schizophrenia was often in the middle of, or triangulated into, parental or family conflict. His training in psychoanalysis certainly added to his sense of remaining neutral in front of the family. Yet it is clear from some of his case studies (Bowen, 1978) that his sense of how the person with schizophrenia was utilized in managing family conflict led him to see the need to help the person with schizophrenia extricate him or herself from such a no-win situation. Perhaps not quite at the level of an open alliance as you would see in structural family therapy, but an alliance nonetheless.

The Genogram

As previously discussed, one way such insights can be gained about the family system is through the use of the genogram. In my own family therapy work with schizophrenia, I have found the genogram an indispensable tool. Often the process of constructing the genogram is a multistage process. First, the family in the therapy session is asked for information to begin building a basic genogram. Second, as part of a homework assignment, each family member is asked to add to or explore parts of the genogram that is still unclear. I often give each family member a copy of the genogram constructed in the session and ask that each add to the genogram as he or she thinks about it over the week. In the next session, the family and I pull together the various additions into a master genogram. In the process, the differences between each family member's reconstruction or additions are discussed. As the family and I explore the multigenerational structure and dynamics, patterns are identified and discussed with regard to how they may be playing out in the current situation. As the family therapy proceeds, I add dynamic information to my genogram, tracking such issues as triangles, conflicts, repeating patterns of behaviors or beliefs, and family myths and stories.

Dealing with Conflict

The person with schizophrenia, as previously mentioned, is often the focus of or in the middle of parental or family conflict. The need in family therapy is to help those who have the conflict deal more directly with one another rather than through the person with schizophrenia. This requires a two-step process. First, through the analysis and interpretation of family behavior in the session, the family therapist can identify the existence of triangulation. Second, the therapist can help reduce the triangulation by joining with the person with schizophrenia and provide support and encouragement to help the person not get pulled into the conflict. Another way the triangulation can be prevented is by active involvement with the two family members and preventing them from bringing in the third person. I have found the alliance with the person with schizophrenia to be, in general, the more effective process. It has the added benefit of empowering the person with schizophrenia to begin to act assertively within the family system.

One outcome of preventing triangulation, encouraging people to deal more directly and effectively with each other, and exploring the family's structural and dynamic history is to begin to address the various levels of differentiation within the family members and between the family members. The goal is to increase the levels of differentiation. Here the theory of Bowen and the reality of what we know about schizophrenia come in to some conflict. Bowen, in his early formulations, felt that extreme levels of poor differentiation, passed on from generation to generation, resulted eventually in someone in the family developing schizophrenia. This simply is not the case. However, poor levels of differentiation can certainly add to the stressful and chaotic environment within which the family, including the person with schizophrenia, exists. Increasing differentiation will not make the schizophrenia go away. It will, however, help stabilize some aspects of the environment.

One way this applies to schizophrenia is to help the family establish some degree of mutual interdependence and appropriate independence within the family system. For example, many families may need to envison their relative with schizophrenia as a thinking, feeling, independent person who has unique needs and desires. I am struck by how some families will talk about their relative with schizophrenia right in front of the individual as if he or she is oblivious to what is being said. At other times, the family and the relative with schizophrenia are so merged together no one can do anything without everyone's involvement. The notion of differentiation in these cases is more about establishing degrees of independence and interdependence (similar to the idea of boundaries in structural family therapy).

The Bowenian concept of *intrapsychic* differentiation, especially for the person with schizophrenia, is perhaps inappropriate. The neurobiology of schizophrenia implies some fundamental miscommunication among emotions, thoughts, and behaviors in many people with this illness. However, the emotional stability and healthy functioning of the parents or caregivers is essential to their long-term involvement in caring for a relative with schizophrenia. Helping the family identify barriers to such emotional health, perhaps due to multigenerational issues and problems in conflict management and decision making, can only add to the stability of the family system.

Conclusion

What lies ahead for Bowenian family therapy in the treatment of schizophrenia? It seems that Bowen's theory still has a role to play in our understanding of how to work effectively with this population. His theoretical concepts of multigenerational processes, family projection process, and triangulation all seem relevant to what family therapists experience in working with families coping with schizophrenia. The work of second and third generation Bowenians, especially in the areas of gender and ethnicity, seem extremely important to future work with families coping with schizophrenia. The influence of gender, sexual orientation, and ethnic background on how certain types of families cope with schizophrenia is critical to our understanding of the family-intervention process. But little is known about many of these factors. Do African-American families cope with schizophrenia the same as Caucasian families? What type of family intervention is best suited to the needs of Asian-American families? How do gay and lesbian couples cope with schizophrenia? What are the unique needs of single-parent families in coping with schizophrenia? Such questions need to be explored by the next generation of family therapists working with schizophrenia. Bowen's theory would provide an important point of departure for such inquiries.

Chapter 5

Experiential Family Therapy

BRIEF OVERVIEW AND APPLICATION TO SCHIZOPHRENIA

Early Pioneers

Experiential family therapy had its beginnings in the life and work of two key figures, Carl Whitaker and Virginia Satir. Although both approached family therapy very differently, they are related in their quest for spontaneity, risk-taking, and an essential humanness in their interactions with families. In watching either of them at work, they seemed to interact with families in much the same way as they would interact with people they met on the street. No difference was evident between their professional and personal selves.

Although the use and development of experiential family therapy dropped off after their deaths, several family and couples therapists continue to use many of their ideas. August Napier, David Keith, and Walter Kempler have written extensively from an experiential perspective. Susan Johnson and Leslie Greenberg have focused on couples therapy from an experiential orientation. With the exception of Carl Whitaker, few of these family clinicians have involved themselves in the treatment of schizophrenia. Therefore, to get a better appreciation for what experiential family therapy is and how it relates to schizophrenia, the focus will be on the work of Carl Whitaker.

Carl Whitaker

Carl Whitaker's medical training was first in obstetrics and gynecology. However, he soon moved into psychiatry. He was taken almost immediately with working with people with psychosis. He became the chairman of the psychiatry department at Emory University where he served from 1946 to 1955. Then, in a provocative move that prefigured his provocative therapy, he and his entire faculty resigned from Emory and set up the Atlanta Psychiatric Clinic. Whitaker remained there until 1965, where he collaborated with Thomas Malone, Richard Felder, and John Warkentin. Experiential therapy was born out of this collaboration. One important book to emerge from this collaboration was *Psychotherapy of Chronic Schizophrenic Patients* (1958), edited by Whitaker. It was a collection of discussions between Malcolm Hayward, Gregory Bateson, John Warkentin, Don Jackson, Thomas Malone, John Rosen, Edward Taylor, and Whitaker. Edward Taylor served as the moderator for the discussion of family management in treating schizophrenia.

In 1965, Whitaker moved to the University of Wisconsin at Madison where he remained until his retirement in the late 1980s. His work on family therapy with schizophrenia was included in *Intensive Family Therapy: Theoretical and Practical Aspects* (Ivan Boszormenyi-Nagy and James Framo, 1965), and *Family Therapy: Theory and Practice* (Guerin, 1976). Whitaker co-authored two classic books on experiential family therapy. In 1978 Augustus Napier and Whitaker wrote *The Family Crucible*. In 1988 Whitaker and William Bumberry wrote *Dancing with the Family: A Symbolic Experiential Approach*. Much of Whitaker's writings were pulled together in 1982 in *From Psyche to System: The Evolving Therapy of Carl Whitaker*, edited by Neill and Kniskern.

Carl Whitaker died in 1995. Throughout his life, he maintained a strong interest in working with families coping with schizophrenia. His provocative style and eccentric behavior, at least in the early part of his career, certainly got him noticed. His basic humanity and compassion for people with schizophrenia made him an influential family therapy leader to people working with this population. He was a tireless lecturer and trainer, often willing to demonstrate his model to groups across the country.

Battle for Structure

Several critical components emerge from his writings about his family therapy work with schizophrenia. Although Whitaker was known for saying and doing odd and provocative things in therapy, there was a system behind his often spontaneous family therapy activity. One critical component to Whitaker's therapy was the idea of the battle for structure (Whitaker and Keith, 1981). This battle involves the therapist trying to establish control over the family therapy from the beginning. Such control is achieved by specifying who must attend the session, how the session will run, and establishing ground rules about the family's participation in therapy. From Whitaker's standpoint, such control is a necessity for establishing a focus to the therapy, one that is established by the therapist.

In working with families coping with schizophrenia, very often there is a "fix the ill person" mentality. In some families, the non-mentally ill family members may see their participation as marginal or even unnecessary. If they do attend the family sessions, it is often to just share information about the person with schizophrenia. The notion of the family system as a whole and each person's role in the system is often disregarded (or not believed). In my own work with these families, such a notion is directly confronted and established when I require the whole family to attend the first therapy session. One outcome of this process is the shift in focus from exclusively the person with schizophrenia to encompassing the entire family.

Battle for Initiative

Once the battle for structure is established, the therapist must then contend with the battle for initiative (Whitaker and Keith, 1981). Whitaker felt he had a role to play in helping families achieve their goals, thus his need for control to establish such a role. He also had a profound respect for the autonomy of the family. The battle for initiative focuses on allowing the family the freedom to determine the course of therapy, and respecting the family's right to its own destiny, both inside and outside of therapy. If the family gives some element of control over to the therapist, there can be a desire to then turn the whole process over to the therapist. Some families may see the therapist as the expert and simply wait for the therapist to diagnose what is wrong and then recommend a solution. The family takes no initiative in establishing the goals of therapy and sees itself as a passive participant in the process. Whitaker made sure each family understood that nothing would be accomplished without the family taking some initiative in what it wanted to accomplish and how the goals were to be achieved once the therapy was begun.

In some cases, this notion of initiative prefigures some of the strengths-based approaches to family therapy, and parallels some of the ideas in solution-oriented family therapy. In working with families coping with schizophrenia, initiative is a key element. Many families are burned out from caring for or confused about how to manage the person with schizophrenia. They come to therapy expecting to hear from an expert who will tell them exactly what to do. By resisting the impulse to lecture and advise these families, the therapist pushes the family toward a more active and collaborative participation in the therapy.

Alienation

Whitaker established the context of the therapy, and the family established the content. One element that Whitaker was very focused on was the experience of alienation. He saw families as emotional systems; each person had his or her emotional life, and the family as a whole created a shared emotional environment within which the family existed. Alienation is the experience of being shut off from true feelings, to have one's emotional life buried under defenses or seen as a dangerous facet of the personality. The idea of alienation is similar to Bowen's notion of an emotional cutoff. A person who is cut off or alienated from his or her emotional life cannot achieve intimacy with others in the family.

Emotional Expression

Many of Whitaker's provocative comments and questions were designed to reach or free up the person's emotional experience of life. Emotional expression is difficult for many families coping with schizophrenia. For one, the concept of expressed emotion has been linked to relapse in schizophrenia. Although expressed emotion has specific components (e.g., intrusiveness and overt criticism), it still raises the concern about the nature of the emotional environment within which the person with schizophrenia exists. How much emotion is appropriate? What are appropriate emotions to express? What behaviors emerge when the individual is fearful of expressing emotions? Parents and caregivers are emotional beings, as is the person with schizophrenia, and not expressing emotions, or becoming alienated from that part of life, can lead to problematic behaviors.

Many families coping with schizophrenia need a place in which they can reconnect to the emotional experiences of their lives and see how such emotional experiences may be tied into their relationship with the person with schizophrenia. I have worked with many families in which individuals seem emotionally distant from one another. They seem to think that such emotional deadness is a better environment for the person with schizophrenia, that it is less chaotic. Unfortunately, these individuals often harbor intense emotional reactions that remain bottled up inside leading to misdirected emotional outbursts on one extreme, or to severe emotional withdrawal on the other.

One way to free up this emotional life is to help families engage in "craziness" (Whitaker and Ryan, 1989), the nonrational, creative functioning believed to reside on the right side of the brain. Whitaker saw this as imperative for healthy functioning for both the family and the therapist. His use of provocative and odd statements and questions in therapy accessed this functioning and demonstrated its usefulness. In this sense, the therapist becomes the role model for the families, freeing up this playful side to their thinking and feeling.

In family therapy with schizophrenia, many clients overrationalize or create an environment of intellectual rigidity as a way of coping with the chaos stirred up by the symptoms of schizophrenia. Such rigidity often gets in the way of spontaneously coping with problems that arise within the family in the process of coping with the illness. Whitaker tried to demonstrate how accessing this side of functioning could free up the family to find new and creative ways of responding to the person with schizophrenia or find new solutions to problems previously thought intractable.

Some families who experience a reduction in their anxiety level or a freeing up of some emotional experiences may, according to Whitaker and Ryan (1989), have a "flight into health." A family may flee therapy prematurely once their anxiety is reduced or some small goal is attained. Whitaker did not see such flight as a negative event, and did not take steps to prevent it. He felt many families would return to therapy and be at a different place emotionally due to the changes that occurred that prompted the flight in the first place. He saw no need to penalize the families or make them feel guilty.

Families coping with schizophrenia often engage in such flight. It is often precipitated by a sense that some small change has occurred and that the family now has what it needs to cope with the illness.

Sometimes such flight is necessary for the family to regroup and adjust to change. Therapists should be somewhat flexible in this process and not see such flight as a sign of underlying pathology or a sign of resistance.

ESSENTIAL SKILLS AND TECHNIQUES

Whitaker's main skill was his personality and style of interaction with the family. For this reason, many family therapists who have tried to copy his style by watching Whitaker in action often fail with their families. Although it is not possible to become a mini-Whitaker, there are several skills that a family therapist can engage in and filter through his or her own style.

Much of Whitaker's work was designed to access the emotional experiences and life of the family. Getting to these emotional experiences was a requirement for the family to progress in a healthier fashion. The alienation from such emotional life was the key factor in family difficulty. Resistance to accessing these emotional experiences was met by Whitaker head on. He would cajole, provoke, seduce, and, at times, display his own "craziness" in an attempt to free up the family and allow the individual members and the family as a whole to reconnect with their emotions. Although the true and honest expression of emotions can be experienced by some families coping with schizophrenia as dangerous, disconnecting or withdrawing from emotions prevents the family from coping adequately with the illness. Whitaker was less concerned with a specific technique that would break down this resistance. He was more interested in the therapist seeing the necessity for accessing emotional experiences and using himself or herself as the major tool to accomplish this task.

Encounters

Whitaker could judge if the task was being accomplished if an encounter took place. An encounter occurred if two people dropped their defenses and interacted honestly with each other, either family member to family member or family member to therapist. Whitaker would often engage in this behavior with specific family members both as a way of modeling such encounters and as an attempt to help the family member begin accessing his or her own emotional experiences. Such emotionally honest dialogue between the therapist and family member was certainly controversial, and often appeared confrontational to onlookers. But for Whitaker it seemed to work.

For families coping with schizophrenia, such honesty in expression toward other family members, especially the person with schizophrenia, can be viewed as dangerous. Fear of conflict, of setting the person with schizophrenia off into a rage or decompensation, or of increasing the emotional intensity within the family are resisted, often for good reason. Yet the emotional climate is an important facet of a healthy family. For families with a member with schizophrenia it is probably more realistic to see the issue of emotional encounters on a continuum. The therapist may help the family find a balance in its ability to express feelings more openly and appropriately, and maintain a healthy atmosphere for the person with schizophrenia.

Personal Involvement

Whitaker felt the only way to achieve such encounters was for the therapist to be personally involved. Personal involvement meant the therapist must be a real, involved, and caring person. If no such personal involvement was present, then no real learning could occur. Whitaker's use of self-disclosure was a way to increase his personal involvement with the family. Although self-disclosure is sometimes seen as a controversial procedure in therapy, many families respond warmly to such revelations that indicate the therapist is a human being with thoughts, feelings, reactions, and a history. There are no clear guidelines about what should or should not be revealed; it is usually up to the therapist to set the appropriate boundary. Whitaker, at least early in his career, was probably more self-disclosing than most.

THE PROCESS OF FAMILY THERAPY

It is difficult to discuss how experiential family therapy with schizophrenia would proceed. This is due primarily to Whitaker's reluctance to map out a model replete with techniques and stages of action. Yet in many ways, his family therapy is the easiest to comprehend. His focus on process was to concentrate on being with and experiencing the family. Whitaker wanted to sit in a room and get a feel for who the family was, how it functioned, and how its members related on an emotional level with one another. Such an intense personal experience allowed Whitaker to develop a real sense of its emotional landscape. The activity the therapist engages in to get to this sense was of less importance to Whitaker.

In working with families coping with schizophrenia from an experiential orientation, the therapist would focus initially on getting the entire family in for a meeting and then turn things over to the family. It would be less focused on technique and more focused on particular areas of the family and how to understand those areas. The therapist would want to focus primarily on family self-awareness and the emotional expression available within the family. With the presence of schizophrenia in the family, emotional expression often runs the extremes from almost absent to overly chaotic and confrontational. Neither extreme is healthy for the family as a whole.

Confrontation

For families in which emotional expression is almost absent, the therapist can use one or two experiences (rather than label them techniques) to engender some emotional activity in the family. First, the therapist may select confrontation. Confrontation can take several different forms depending on the strength of the family and the talent of the therapist. *Direct confrontation* can be comments made to individuals within the family or to the family as a whole that provoke comment and emotional reaction from the family. The comments can be in the form of a rhetorical question, a statement of fact, or an observation about the family. It is important to remember that each family has its own internal strength to handle such confrontation. The therapist should only use direct confrontation when he or she has formed some assessment of the family's strength.

A second form of confrontation that can be used, especially with families whose strength to handle direct confrontation is limited, is more indirect and utilizes more subtle questions and *hypothesis testing*. The questions are often focused on possible areas of resistance to open expression. Hypothesis testing is when the therapist offers his or her own internal thinking about the family, what he or she sees, believes, and how the therapist is organizing his or her thoughts about the family. In my work with families coping with schizophrenia I try to phrase such hypotheses in a way that invites dialogue or challenge from the family. I might say, "Correct me if I'm wrong, but what I'm seeing makes me think . . .", or "You might not agree with this, but I think. . . ." At times, my statements are meant to be absurd or provocative in order to ensure an argument from the family. An argument is one type of emotional expression that often leads to more open communication within the family.

Use of Exercises

For families in which the emotional expression is chaotic or confrontational, the therapist can use exercises as a way of modeling healthier emotional expression. In guiding families through problem-solving exercises, role-plays, and naturalistic experiences through homework assignments, the family members can learn how to better manage and focus their use of emotional expression. The therapist can model such appropriate emotional expression by helping the family establish ground rules for the therapy sessions and aligning with family members who may be the focus of intense or hostile emotional expression. Such an alliance often changes the balance of power in the family and forces the family to rethink how it manages its emotional life.

Conclusion

What does the future hold for experiential family therapy in the treatment of schizophrenia? The future is probably somewhat dim. Whitaker's model of family therapy had noble aspirations in trying to help families create a sense of togetherness, genuineness, emotional honesty, and increased self-esteem. However, the emotional intensity of the model probably does not fit well with the illness of schizophrenia. The use of confrontation, although fine for some families, may not be well received by families stressed out and fractured from dealing with schizophrenia. Whitaker focused on the importance of emotional expression and emotional intimacy in families. As we increase our knowledge about schizophrenia, the role of family environment, and the role of expressed emotions in families, better models achieve some of the same ends as Whitaker's model but do so in a more supportive fashion. Still, Whitaker's use of self, how he put himself on the line with the families, and his deep compassion for people struggling with schizophrenia are all attitudes and behaviors many family therapists interested in working with schizophrenia can learn from.

Chapter 6

Structural Family Therapy

BRIEF OVERVIEW AND APPLICATION TO SCHIZOPHRENIA

Salvador Minuchin

Salvador Minuchin is considered the primary theoretician and technician of structural family therapy. Growing out of his work with multiproblem children and their families in the 1950s and 1960s, Minuchin developed a theory of family therapy that is both concrete in its techniques and comprehensive in its scope of both etiology and treatment. His theoretical and technical writing has always been very accessible, making his theory very attractive to novice family therapists. Minuchin was trained at the William Allison White Institute, where he was schooled in the work of Harry Stack Sullivan. He went to the Wiltwyck School for delinquent boys, where he focused on multiproblem children and their families. There he collaborated with Dick Auerswald, Braulio Montalvo, Charles King, and Clara Rabinowitz. Out of his work at Wiltwyck came the first attempt at presenting structural family therapy in *Families of the Slums* (1967). Minuchin became director of the Philadelphia Child Guidance Center in 1965. Some of the colleagues who worked with Minuchin at the Center included Montalvo, Jay Haley, Harry Aponte, Charles Fishman, and Cloe Madanes. In 1974, Minuchin published the highly influential book, *Families and Family Therapy.* This book put structural family therapy on the map, making it one of the most popular forms of family therapy. This was followed by the publication of *Psychosomatic Families: Anorexia Nervosa in Context* (1978). This book presented empirical support for structural family therapy, a type of support missing from the literature for many other types of family therapy. Minuchin eventually left the center and began his own center in New

York. He retired in 1996. He is still an active clinician, lecturer, and trainer in family therapy. Some of his more active followers include Harry Aponte, Jorge Colapinto, and Michael Nichols. Minuchin did not work extensively with schizophrenia. His 1974 book makes only one mention of a case of a fourteen-year-old boy with a schizophrenic breakdown. However, structural family therapy has been very influential in the field and many of its concepts are applicable to working with families coping with schizophrenia.

Boundaries

One of the major concepts of structural family therapy was the understanding of boundaries (Minuchin, 1974). Boundaries are the psychological, emotional, behavioral, and relational ties that outline the family and separate one family from another. A healthy functioning family will have a clearly delineated sense of itself, and it will know who its members are and how it is different from other families. Boundaries exist on a continuum, with healthy families having strong boundaries that help self-identification, but flexible boundaries that allow for change during the family's life span. At either end of the continuum are the unhealthy boundary types. On one extreme is the disengaged family. Here the family has developed very rigid boundaries making communication between members or subgroups within the family very difficult. On the other extreme is the enmeshed family. Here the family develops very diffuse boundaries between members making differentiation difficult.

In family therapy with schizophrenia, often the presence of schizophrenia has led the family to move toward one extreme type of boundary or the other. In my practice I tend to see the enmeshed family boundary system more often. Such a system is often generated out of concern for the person with schizophrenia. But that concern can lead to intrusiveness and inappropriate concern. The person with schizophrenia may experience a lack of individuality within the family. He or she may feel no power or ability to make even minor decisions for himself or herself.

Coalitions

Another primary concept of structural family therapy is the coalition (Minuchin, 1974). A coalition is usually a covert alliance between two people against a third. This is similar to Bowen's notion of triangulation. In family therapy with schizophrenia, coalitions often take one of two forms. First, the person with schizophrenia may be the target of the coalition formed by two other family members. The person with schizophrenia may feel isolated, marginalized, or powerless in the family. Second, the person with schizophrenia may be in an alliance with another family member against a third person. Often, the person with schizophrenia and a parent may form an alliance, essentially distancing the other parent or excluding the parent from their relationship. Such an alliance may be initially based on genuine concern for the person with schizophrenia and how he or she is treated in the family. If the person with schizophrenia is seen as the target for hostile comments or serves as the scapegoat in the family, one parent may form an alliance to try to balance things out. This can work fine as long as the alliance does not become a covert dynamic used against the other members of the family.

Detouring

Structural family therapy addresses the concept of detouring (Minuchin, 1974). Detouring occurs when the stresses between parents or caregivers get redirected through a child so the subsystem of the parents or caregivers seems more stable. Detouring shares some similarities with triangulation and the family projection process discussed by Bowen (see Chapter 4). In families coping with schizophrenia, the person with schizophrenia often becomes the focus of attention and concern, and often the focus for anger and resentment. Although the nature of schizophrenia can engender such concern and emotions, sometimes the emotions are misdirected and indicate a problem between the parents or caregivers. The person with schizophrenia is simply an easy target to explain the family's difficulty. Often this dynamic is revealed in statements by family members directed at the person with schizophrenia, such as "If you were better we wouldn't have all these problems" or "The only reason we argue is because of your illness."

Hierarchy

The concept of hierarchy addresses the boundary that differentiates the leader from other members of the family (Minuchin, 1974). In healthy families, it is supposed that the parents are in a clear hierarchy and lead the family. Problems arise when other subsystems emerge as the leader. A family coping with schizophrenia faces a potential hierarchy problem when the illness of schizophrenia becomes the dominant force or controlling mechanism within the family. Although the parents may seem to be in control, they make decisions or engage in behaviors based on how the person with schizophrenia may respond. I have had parents tell me such things as, "We couldn't go on a vacation this year because our son may need us," or "We didn't want to change the house too much and worry our son, so we put off painting." Again, such concern may start out with the best intentions. But it may lead to the illness of schizophrenia taking control of the family. Narrative family therapists have addressed this dynamic as well.

Subsystems

A final concept critical to structural family therapy is the subsystem (Minuchin, 1974). A subsystem is a unit within a family. Sometimes subsystems are naturally occurring, such as the subsystem of children or the subsystem of the women in the family. At other times, subsystems may be the result of a particular alliance created by some members of the family. In a family coping with schizophrenia, subsystems may be created to contend with the periodic difficulty brought on by the illness. In other cases, the person with schizophrenia may be part of a subsystem as a way for that person to have a voice in the family if he or she has been marginalized. The family therapist needs to recognize the existence and dynamics behind the formation of subsystems and how they add to the homeostasis of the family.

ESSENTIAL SKILLS AND TECHNIQUES

Minuchin (1974) was very careful to outline his approach to family therapy and the essential skills needed to reach a successful end. For this reason, many new family therapists are drawn to his model and find it very user friendly. Minuchin was a good technician, and although his model has not been used extensively with schizophrenia, his techniques have some utility with this population.

Accommodation

Accommodation was the primary technique that allows the therapist to engage the family and proceed with therapy (Minuchin, 1974). It is the adjustment a therapist makes in order to build an alliance with the family. The adjustments include several interrelated processes. *Joining* is the process of establishing a rapport with the family. Such rapport helps the therapist become, at least temporarily, part of the family. *Maintenance* involves the behaviors and attitudes the therapist portrays that help continue the rapport with the family. *Mimesis* is the process of paralleling the family's mood or behavior. The therapist may adjust his or her voice tone, language, posture, or body language to reflect that used by the family.

In work with families coping with schizophrenia, building a trusting relationship is a prerequisite to effective intervention. Often, these families have a history of poor experiences with therapists and doctors and may be hesitant to get involved with another professional. Many models of family intervention with schizophrenia focus on the need to join with the family and be viewed as supporting the family. Structural family therapy simply breaks this need down into small and manageable steps. Accommodation helps the therapist see the transactional patterns within the family.

Enactment

Minuchin (1974) felt one way to identify problematic transactional patterns in a family was through enactment. Enactment is the acting out of the dysfunctional transactional patterns within a family therapy session. Minuchin believed acting out should be encouraged by the therapist. In many cases, the dynamics of the family will lead to acting out in the therapist's presence without much activity by the therapist. However, such occurrences must be treated carefully when working with families coping with schizophrenia. Individuals with schizophrenia can be very sensitive and reactive to the behavior of others. Many families try hard to prevent acting-out behavior for fear it will set off the person with schizophrenia. The therapist must provide some safety, guidance, and debriefing if acting out occurs within the therapy session.

Boundary Marking

Since structural family therapy focuses on family boundaries, one technique developed by Minuchin (1974) addresses the need to alter problematic boundaries. Boundary marking refers to the therapist's attempts to reinforce appropriate boundaries and diffuse inappropriate boundaries by changing the transactional patterns within the family. One of the primary goals of structural family therapy is the development of healthy and adaptive family boundaries. Such boundaries need to be responsive to the family's needs across time and across situations. For families coping with schizophrenia, the boundaries must support their coping with a potentially chronic and severe mental illness, and also allow for family growth and change across the life span of the family. However, since the person with schizophrenia is not incapacitated severely all of the time, in many cases, the nature of the family boundaries must be flexible to respond to periodic crises and solid enough to establish a healthy identity to support individual development.

Restructuring

Restructuring is another technique developed by Minuchin (1974) to help change family boundaries. This is essentially a generic term for any intervention that confronts a family and facilitates structural change. One example he used was *unbalancing*. The therapist would support one member of the family through an overt alliance, thus interfering with the family's homeostasis. In families coping with schizophrenia, often the person with schizophrenia has been marginalized or scapegoated by the family. When the therapist sides with this person in an overt alliance, it not only causes the family to struggle with maintaining the status quo, but it also provides some needed support and power to the person with schizophrenia. Such support and power may be critical for the person to feel that his or her needs are understood.

THE PROCESS OF FAMILY THERAPY

Joining

The process of structural family therapy in the treatment of schizophrenia follows the general outline provided by Minuchin (1974). In fact, some suggestions within the structural family therapy framework are also found in behavioral and psychoeducational models of intervention. The first step in the process is joining with the family. Through the techniques associated with accommodation, the therapist seeks to form a working alliance with the family. Often, families coping with schizophrenia may bring to this activity a history of problematic interactions with other mental health professionals. The therapist will need to be sensitive to each family's history of seeking help and understand its level of anxiety, stigma, and fear and how these emotions interact. In many cases, joining is not a discrete task accomplished within the first one or two sessions, but an ongoing process throughout the family therapy experience. The therapist must always attend to the relationship with the family.

The Contract

The second step in the process is the development of a contract. This can be a formal or an informal process. Minuchin (1974) noted that many families come into treatment with a very specific goal in mind. In many cases, the therapist needs to help the family broaden its understanding of what family therapy can accomplish and what needs of the family are not being met. In working with families coping with schizophrenia, often the stated goal is to fix the person with schizophrenia. This is obviously beyond the scope of any model of family therapy. However, families can learn better coping skills, develop better structures to help them cope with the stresses brought on by the illness, develop better boundaries to help facilitate each family member's ability to function, and to help the entire family adapt and grow both internally and in relation to the larger social environment. In some cases, the goals may be more focused on how to live with or change a specific behavioral pattern in the family.

The Restructuring Process

When a contract has been discussed and formed, the therapist develops information about the nature of the family's structure, boundaries, and transactional patterns. Careful questioning, observing the family members' interactions, taking note of acting-out experiences, and the assignment of tasks (homework assignments either carried out in or outside the session) can bring much of this information to the front. Once the therapist has formed some hypotheses, he or she determines where to help the family begin the restructuring process.

The bulk of family therapy involves the restructuring process. Through the use of alliances, homework, manipulating subsystems, and other targeted interventions, the therapist challenges the family's status quo and brings to light alternative ways for them to relate to each other through changes in the family structure. A change in structure can lead to a change in the transactional patterns. A change in the transactional patterns can lead to the elimination of some problematic behaviors or feelings or the development of new and positive behaviors and feelings.

In working with families coping with schizophrenia, I have found that many develop very rigid ways of handling stress and crises. They often marginalize the person with schizophrenia in the belief that it will decrease the stress the person experiences. Or they will focus all their time and emotion on the person with schizophrenia in an attempt to provide what they believe to be the right kind of care. Sometimes, such care is motivated out of guilt or shame. In other cases, the family firmly believes that if the person with schizophrenia could just change then the entire family would be happier and function better. Although any of these scenarios is understandable given what families have to cope with when living with schizophrenia, the outcome is a rigid, nonadaptive family structure that has difficulty responding to individual family member needs and the needs of the family across time. The process of structural family therapy provides one avenue to change some of these elements and increase coping.

Conclusion

What does the future hold for structural family therapy's role in treating schizophrenia? It would seem the future is guardedly optimistic. Optimistic in the sense that structural family therapy has some empirical support for its effectiveness with difficult family issues such as anorexia nervosa. It is unfortunate that more practitioners of structural family therapy have not applied the model to schizophrenia. Recently, Minuchin, Colapinto, and Minuchin (1998) and Aponte (1994) have applied the model to multiproblem and poor families, two populations who share some issues in common with families coping with schizophrenia. One of the strengths of the structural model is its clear and logical flow from theory to model to technique. It is an untapped resource and has been underutilized in the family treatment of schizophrenia.

Chapter 7

Strategic Family Therapy

BRIEF OVERVIEW AND APPLICATION TO SCHIZOPHRENIA

Early Pioneers

Strategic family therapy developed out of direct clinical work and research on schizophrenia. It emerged from Gregory Bateson's early work in Palo Alto, California, on family communication and schizophrenia. Jay Haley, John Weakland, and Don Jackson joined Bateson and continued the focus on schizophrenia and communication. Out of this collaboration came the influential notion of the double-bind hypothesis of communication in families with a relative with schizophrenia.

Don Jackson continued this line of work at the Mental Research Institute (MRI) in Palo Alto, which he founded in 1959. Jay Haley, John Weakland, Paul Watzlawick, and Richard Fisch joined him there. Through the influence of Haley, some of the critical theoretical and practical work of Milton Erickson was incorporated into this developing model of family therapy. The MRI established one of the first training programs in family therapy.

These collaborations resulted in several important publications on strategic therapy. In particular, *Strategies of Psychotherapy* (Haley, 1963) and *Pragmatics of Human Communication* (Watzlawick, Beavin, and Jackson, 1967) helped put strategic family therapy on the map. Haley continued to promote it in his 1987 book, *Problem-Solving Therapy*. Cloe Madanes, another major strategic family therapist who collaborated with Haley, wrote the influential book *Strategic Family Therapy* (1981).

In 1967 the MRI developed a Brief Therapy Center under the direction of Richard Fisch. More will be said about this specific program in the following text. This discussion of strategic family therapy and its usefulness with schizophrenia will focus on the work of Haley and Madanes.

Several key concepts emerge from the strategic family therapy work of Haley and Madanes and the early work of Gregory Bateson and his colleagues at Palo Alto that have some direct relevance to working with people with schizophrenia. In many cases, the concepts focus on individual and family communication. These include the concepts of metacommunication, the double bind, and the differentiation between metaphorical or symbolic messages and content messages. Although these concepts no longer apply to explaining the etiology of schizophrenia, they can provide important insights into the functioning of families coping with schizophrenia.

Metacommunication

Metacommunication is really communication about communication. It generally applies to *covert* or nonverbal messages that are sent in tandem with *overt* or verbal messages. Such covert messages include voice tone and body language that may imply how a person is supposed to understand the more direct verbal messages. In family therapy with schizophrenia, such metacommunication occurs frequently. In fact, it happens in all families all of the time. In the best of all possible worlds, the overt messages and the covert messages are in synch. When a family member says to another family member, "I love you," the words are usually matched with good eye contact and a warmth and genuineness in the voice tone. But at other times, especially in families under stress or experiencing a crisis, the communication can become skewed. Statements such as "Do what you want," are conveyed with the body language and voice tone that implies, "As long as it's what I want, too." The difficulty with families coping with schizophrenia is that the person with schizophrenia may be unable to pick up on such skewed communication and fail to appreciate the difference between the overt and covert messages. If the person with schizophrenia then acts on the direct or overt messages, he or she may be met with hostility or rejection and a sense of failure to do the right thing.

Double Bind

One type of extreme situation where the metacommunication is skewed is referred to as the double bind. As originally proposed by Bateson and his colleagues, the double bind includes an overt message that is contradicted by the covert message, such skewed communication takes place within an emotionally close relationship, and the person on the receiving end of the message cannot comment on the contradiction of the messages. In families in which the boundaries are diffuse or there is poor differentiation between members the emotional intensity can lead to such extreme skewed communication. Although Bateson felt the double bind was critical to the etiology of schizophrenia, this is no longer the case. However, as an example of how communication can go wrong in a family, it still seems to have some validity as a concept. The critical piece in working with families coping with schizophrenia is the third ingredient of the double bind, the inability to comment on the contradiction being experienced. Many people with schizophrenia are unable to point out experiences of confused or contradictory communication. At times, the confused communication can become endemic to the family as a whole.

Metaphorical versus Symbolic Messages

The differentiation between metaphorical or symbolic messages and the direct content of messages is related to understanding metacommunication and the double bind. Strategic family therapists refer to a symbolic or metaphorical message as an *analogical* message. Direct content is called a *digital* message. In some cases, the metaphorical or symbolic message can be in the form of a behavior. In either case, the metaphor refers to the broader meaning of the direct message. In some families coping with schizophrenia, the process of communication becomes muddled and confused on many levels. In my work with such families (Marley, 1992, 1999), I have found it important to help them both listen carefully to their direct messages and also consider the possible metaphoric or symbolic meaning of the messages.

Other interrelated concepts from strategic family therapy focus on family behavior. These concepts include circular causality, homeostasis, and first-order and second-order change. Many of these concepts have their origins in the early cybernetic theories of Bateson and his colleagues at Palo Alto, which explains the choice of language in labeling and explaining these concepts.

Circular Causality

Circular causality is a critical concept in strategic family therapy. Rather than seeing behavior in a family as a linear cause-and-effect process, the strategic family therapist sees the behavior as indicative of a repetitive cycle the family engages in. In a family coping with schizophrenia this can be a difficult idea to explore without conveying a sense of blame on one or more members of the family. Often, the family will say, "Our son just gets so angry and won't take his meds. Then we get all upset and I can't sleep. If only he would take his meds things would be better." The linear notion is if the son takes his medication then the family will be doing better. From a strategic perspective, the anger and resistance to medication is simply one point on a cycle that involves the whole family. But this can come across as blaming the parents for the son's anger. The need to seek and identify a fundamental point of cause, the event that leads to all other events, is strong in families who often feel marginalized, powerless, or under attack by mental health professionals. Circular causality is not an attempt to seek the origin of the illness, but an attempt to broaden the scope of how to understand the occurrence of certain repetitive behaviors in the family.

Homeostasis

The concept of homeostasis is defined by Piercy and associates (1996) as, "The tendency within a system to seek equilibrium or balance through maintaining the status quo and resisting change. Theorists differ as to whether family pathology is maintained by resisting change (homeostasis or negative feedback) or by engaging in vicious cycles of change-attempting behavior (positive feedback or error amplification)" (p. 60). Circular causality becomes the context within which the family homeostasis is established and maintained. Many families coping with schizophrenia achieve a certain degree of homeostasis. As previously mentioned, the balance may be achieved at the cost to one member of the family. The role of the identified patient, the scapegoat, or the sick role are all interrelated and identify a family function necessary to the maintenance of family balance.

First-Order and Second-Order Change

Two final concepts focus on family-level behavior. First-order change implies that some behavior in the family has changed but the overall family system remains the same. Second-order change indicates the family behavior has changed and the entire family system has been altered. Often, therapists misinterpret first-order change and feel the family has made great progress only to be disillusioned when it begins to struggle again. The goal of strategic family therapy is to establish a new system for the family to operate within. Achieving such a second-order change requires the entire family system to change, not just the individual behavior of one or two members.

In family therapy with schizophrenia, the person with schizophrenia may decide to start taking his or her medication. However, if the person still does not believe he or she has an illness and if the family still needs a scapegoat to focus on, it is unlikely that taking the medication will fundamentally alter the family system. Such a scenario frequently ends with the person again refusing to take medication and precipitating an individual and family crisis.

Relapse and rehospitalization, not uncommon when working with people struggling with schizophrenia, may indicate that second-order change has still not occurred. Although some current research on schizophrenia cautions against making too bold a claim for family system issues causing relapse, the research on phenomena such as expressed emotion and interpersonal interaction (Marley, 1998) does indicate the possible interaction between family system behavior and communication and relapse in people with schizophrenia.

ESSENTIAL SKILLS AND TECHNIQUES

The goal of strategic family therapy becomes one of working toward second-order change. Although a number of techniques can help achieve this goal, several techniques in particular are found most often in strategic family therapy. Strategic family therapy had some aspects of its origin in working with people with schizophrenia, and some of the techniques would not be considered appropriate given what we now know about schizophrenia.

Reframing

One technique that is useful in family therapy with schizophrenia is the use of reframing. Reframing involves the use of language to rename or relabel a situation or a behavior. By reframing how it experiences a behavior or situation, a family can alter how it deals with the situation or behavior. One example of a reframe at a larger level is the change in how people refer to individuals with schizophrenia. Calling people "schizophrenics" has been reframed as "people with schizophrenia." The change has caused families and professionals to see the illness of schizophrenia as simply a part of the person, not as a reference for the whole person. A family may label or define problems in a way that reifies the illness or marginalizes the individual with schizophrenia to a sick role. Often such definitions diminish a family's ability to see change as possible. Some might say, "Well, he has a chronic mental illness. Doesn't that mean there's nothing we can do?" The family therapist can help the family reframe its definition or sense of the person with the illness, often illuminating areas of change and help in the process.

Directives

A second technique used in strategic family therapy is the use of directives. These are tasks assigned by the therapist for the family to carry out. In the process of carrying out the directive, or attempting to negotiate how to carry out the directive, the family must interact, often in new ways that demonstrate possible second-order change. Directives have changed over the years with evolving notions of power and collaboration between the therapist and the family. Early on, directives seemed to represent the therapist as a powerful taskmaster who used professional superiority to get the family to attempt change. Later, strategic therapists looked on directives as a more collaborative process that involved extensive knowledge of the family and what it had tried in the past to effect change.

Paradox, Ordeals, and Pretending

Three techniques used in strategic family therapy would not be considered appropriate for the treatment of schizophrenia. These are therapeutic paradox, prescribing ordeals, and pretending. Given our current knowledge of schizophrenia these techniques would be counterproductive and possibly harmful to the person with schizophrenia and his or her family. The use of paradox involves the implementation of a seemingly illogical or contrary intervention. Ordeals, as a type of directive, involve assigning an unpleasant task to be carried out each time the symptomatic behavior is engaged in. Pretending involves asking the individual to pretend to engage in the symptomatic behavior that reframes the behavior as under the person's control. One of the problems with these types of techniques as they apply to working with people with schizophrenia is the use of deception. People with schizophrenia may, due to their illness, be suspicious of people and have difficulty understanding the nuances of some communication and behavior on either the therapist or the family's part. Each of these three techniques has the potential to confuse or provoke a person with schizophrenia given his or her symptoms and coping skills. Also, many families who try to cope with schizophrenia are already dealing with often confusing environments. To ask these families to purposely inject a level of confusion into their environment seems to be asking too much of them.

THE PROCESS OF FAMILY THERAPY

Although some of the techniques of strategic family therapy may be problematic for working with families coping with schizophrenia, the model does have a nice structure to its process that many therapists and families respond well to. Similar to structural family therapy, the structure of this process makes it an easy to understand model, especially for new family therapists.

The Social Stage

Different strategic family therapists utilize different structures to the process of therapy. Haley often broke down the process of family therapy into the social, problem, interactional, and goal-setting stages. The social stage involves allowing family members to relax, get comfortable, and adjust to the new environment. The family is made to feel welcome, and the therapist is already hard at work observing the interactions between family members. This initial process works well for most families, including those coping with schizophrenia. These families may present in an anxious or defensive state, expecting to be blamed for the illness or behavior of the person with schizophrenia. The family may have had prior problematic experiences with mental health professionals. Giving the family a chance to adjust and relax can help alleviate some of this anticipatory anxiety. Plus, it is just a polite thing to do.

The Problem Stage

The social stage is followed by the problem stage. In this stage the therapist explores with each family member his or her perspective of the problem. The therapist tries to obtain some definition and scope of the problem from the family members and begins to assess the types of behaviors that may help maintain the problem. Because Haley was influenced by structural family theory, his process of inquiry with the various family members often had a structural component. Who he would talk to first and how he would address each family member was focused on making structural change in the family from the beginning of therapy. For families coping with schizophrenia, such attention to the perspective of all of the family members can be critical to forming both a therapeutic relationship with the family and to helping the person with schizophrenia feel a part of the process. In some families, the perspective of the person with schizophrenia can become marginalized since he or she is viewed as ill and the source of the problems. The strategic approach, which is mirrored in other approaches, helps guide the therapist toward a process that ensures participation by all family members.

The Interactional Stage

Following the problem stage is the interactional stage. In order to better understand how the family operates both in behavior and communication, Haley would often have families discuss their perspectives of the problems among themselves as he observed their interactions. The process provides a window into the functioning of the family by highlighting many of the concepts previously discussed. Coalitions may become obvious, power differentials may direct how the process unfolds, and issues of triangles and enmeshment might be illuminated through the actions of the family. The overall family patterns that create and maintain family-level problems may show themselves during the discussion. In some ways, this process is the first task or directive used in the strategic therapy. Based on the outcome of this process, the therapist may have a better sense of the goals and objectives of the therapy and can then create more targeted directives for the family to carry out within and between sessions. Such interactional experiences can be very useful when working with families coping with schizophrenia. From a strategic perspective, the interactions give the therapist the best insight into the natural workings of the family. However, given the reactive nature of schizophrenia to stress and chaos, the therapist should maintain some boundaries and control over the interaction if it starts to get out of hand.

Therapeutic Goals

Based on the outcome of the family-interaction process, the therapist can then help the family develop goals and objectives for therapy. In the past, strategic family therapy was more dictatorial in nature and the therapist formed the goals and objectives without family input. Over time, most strategic family therapists have moved toward a more collaborative approach and utilize extensive family input in the creation of goals and objectives.

The need for collaboration is essential when working with families coping with schizophrenia. First, the collaboration helps build a better therapeutic relationship. Second, the collaboration ensures that the person with schizophrenia will have a voice in developing the goals and objectives of the family therapy. The process of "giving voice" to the person with schizophrenia can be a source of empowerment for the individual who may feel marginalized or scapegoated within the family. The family therapy then continues through the use of directives and problem-solving tasks to help the family reach its goals.

Conclusion

What does the future hold for the use of strategic family therapy in the treatment of schizophrenia? The fact that strategic family therapy has laid the foundation for the brief and solution-focused therapies demonstrates it has theoretical and practical strength. It is a robust theory and model with many components that remain useful in working with families. The fact that the model has mellowed over the years and moved away from some of its more radical techniques probably makes it more useful in working with the illness of schizophrenia. Haley's problem-solving approach keeps it somewhat aligned with psychosocial and behavioral family interventions. Unfortunately, with the focus on brief and solution-focused therapies, there may be little interest in studying and researching strategic family therapy in depth as a viable model for working with families coping with schizophrenia. As with some of the other models already discussed, there are many elements of strategic family therapy that can be very effective when working with schizophrenia. Unfortunately, the model has suffered due to its early radical approach and the view that it is an old model with little to offer.

Chapter 8

Systemic/Milan Family Therapy

BRIEF OVERVIEW AND APPLICATION TO SCHIZOPHRENIA

The Milan Group

Systemic family therapy, as practiced by the Milan Group, grew out of the work of Gregory Bateson, Jay Haley, Cloe Madanes, and the MRI. The key individuals in the Milan Group included Mara Selvini Palazzoli, Luigi Boscolo, Gianfranco Cecchin, and Giuliana Prata. Palazzoli was trained as a psychoanalyst and focused on the treatment of anorexia nervosa and schizophrenia. However, she was disenchanted with her individual work and moved more toward a family orientation. In 1971 she and her associates opened the Center for the Study of the Family in Milan, and the Milan model of systemic family therapy was born. In 1978 the group authored the influential book *Paradox and Counterparadox,* which focused on disrupting family homeostasis through the use of paradoxical interventions. In 1980 the Milan Group split into two groups that began divergent work in systemic therapy. Selvini Palazzoli and Prata focused on research. Boscolo and Cecchin focused on training. The work of Boscolo and Cecchin was influential in the development of solution-focused and narrative therapy.

Although the influence of Bateson, Haley, Madanes, and the MRI is apparent in the Milan model of systemic family therapy, some of their major concepts are slightly different and deserve review. Also, many of these concepts emerged from work with families coping with schizophrenia. These concepts include circularity, hypothesis building and curiosity, psychotic family games, and time.

Circularity

Circularity shares some similarity with the strategic family therapy notion of circular causality. However, the Milan Group added a second definition to the concept of circularity. In this definition, the therapist and the family are caught up in a circular relationship. As the therapist interacts with the family, he or she develops hypotheses about the family. The hypotheses lead to specific questions being asked. The answers to the questions lead to new information and a new perspective of the family. This in turn leads to a new hypothesis and new questions. The cycle then repeats itself. This view speaks against the therapist having too many preconceived notions or assumptions about the family. When working with families coping with schizophrenia, it is critical that the therapist is open to changing his or her view of the family based on this circular interaction. However, family therapists are just as prone to misunderstandings or biased beliefs about schizophrenia as are the other family members or the general public. Some of this difficulty can be addressed through training and experience in working with people with schizophrenia.

Hypothesis Building and Curiosity

Hypothesis building and curiosity are interrelated concepts. One has to do with attitude, the other with a process fueled by the attitude. Curiosity is the attitude of the therapist that allows him or her to remain open to multiple understandings or hypotheses about the family. The therapist is not neutral, in the sense of having no theoretical framework to understand what is occurring within the family. However, the therapist should not be constrained by a particular theoretical belief that limits the possible hypotheses he or she entertains in trying to understand the family. Curiosity defines that critical balance between openness to new ideas and being grounded in a particular theoretical orientation that guides the initial activity with a family. The attitude of curiosity promotes the process of hypothesis building. From a systemic/Milan perspective, hypotheses (theories about family functioning) are necessary as they help guide the formation and use of questions. The questions are then used in the circular process previously discussed.

In working with families coping with schizophrenia, I have found it most useful to make my hypothesis building a public process. That is, to think out loud with the family about the hypothesis I am forming about their functioning and what data have gone into the formation of the hypothesis. I often then invite a family critique of the hypothesis. Building on the notion of collaboration, the discussion of the hypothesis allows the family to know what I am thinking about them and invites their input into the creation of a meaningful hypothesis. Also, by making the hypothesis public knowledge, it makes it easier for families to see the connection between tasks or directives I assigned and the goals of the therapy. The hypothesis is the link between the two, but it is a link that for many families is missing from their understanding about the process of family therapy.

Psychotic Family Games

Psychotic family games, although an important interactional process in families, do not carry with them the etiological explanation for the development of psychosis as originally hypothesized by Palazzoli (1986). Research shows that such patterns of interactions do not cause schizophrenia. However, the process involved with these "psychotic" games is one of initially unstable triangles that involve the parents and a child. The child aligns with the loser of the marital conflict. The loser, not seeing the child's behavior for what it is, aligns with the winner of the marital conflict as a way of combating the child's behavior. Eventually, the family system stabilizes around the child's problematic behavior.

In working with families coping with schizophrenia, this process is better understood, I feel, in terms of the motivation and instability of coalitions built within the family. The person with schizophrenia may try to align with a family member who is perceived as sympathetic or available to the person with schizophrenia. Such an alignment may be countered by other family members who see the alignment as counterproductive to the management of the person with schizophrenia. If the family forces a rupture of the alignment, the person with schizophrenia may experience this as a failure on his or her part and as an abandonment on the part of the family member. The person with schizophrenia may show increased signs of symptoms in reaction to the stress of the interaction.

Time

The final concept from systemic/Milan family therapy that is applicable to working with schizophrenia is the notion of time. In many families, how they perceive their current problem may influence how they perceive the past and the future. In a family coping with schizophrenia, if the person with schizophrenia is currently perceived as very ill and the source of all of the family's problems, then the past will be recalled with an emphasis on those events and behaviors that support the current perspective. Likewise, the future will be seen as validating the current perception. Similar to narrative family therapy (see Chapter 10), the therapist must work with the family to get a more accurate picture of the past, one that reflects a broader understanding of the family as a whole. Such a reconstruction can help the family construct a more full understanding of the present and a more hopeful sense of the future.

ESSENTIAL SKILLS AND TECHNIQUES

A number of specific techniques arise from the concepts previously outlined. As with other models of family therapy, some of the techniques may be appropriate for working with families coping with schizophrenia, and others may be counterproductive.

Questions

One of the strengths of the systemic/Milan model is its focus on the use of questions in the process of doing therapy. More so than other models, the early clinicians and theoreticians of this model raised the art of asking good questions almost to a science. The use of *circular* questions became one of the dominant techniques of this model. Unlike many questions asked during family therapy that focus on obtaining new information, circular questions are designed to learn more about changes in the family and differences in the relationships between family members. Such questions are the building blocks for the concepts of circularity and hypothesis building discussed above. With a focus on change and difference, the family therapist gains new insight into the systemic functioning of the family. The new insight leads to new hypotheses that in turn lead to new circular questions. As this process continues, the family can begin to gain insight into its own systemic process.

For families coping with schizophrenia, the attitude of curiosity that helps promote the development and use of circular questions and hypothesis building can be a refreshing environment within which to receive services. The therapist may be the expert in utilizing these techniques, but the family is the expert of its own situation. The therapist uses these techniques to help learn about the idiosyncratic nature of each family and in the process help the family understand what the therapist sees and thinks about the family process. Such a collaborative model of knowledge and hypothesis building counters some of what these families may have experienced in the past with therapists who tried to tell them what to do because the therapist was a supposed expert of all things related to schizophrenia and the family.

Invariant Prescription

A second technique developed by this model was the use of the invariant prescription. Although this technique was developed to counter the development of psychotic family games, it is clear that such family dynamics have nothing to do with the etiology of psychosis or schizophrenia. Nevertheless, the invariant prescription is similar to a structural family therapy intervention that focuses on building a strong coalition between the parents and in the process disrupting other patterns that may have developed due to a weak parental coalition. With the invariant prescription, the parents are asked to form a secret alliance without the rest of the family. The parents may then engage in secret meetings lasting from a few hours to a few days. Such a strong coalition in the midst of the family was believed necessary to disrupt problematic family interactions and patterns.

When working with families coping with schizophrenia, the clinician must be careful with this technique. Certainly, in such families a strong and healthy relationship between the parents or primary caregivers is essential for maintaining good boundaries and sustaining adaptive coping skills. The concern would be on the nature of the secrecy of the coalition and the possible reaction the person with schizophrenia may have to it. In many families coping with schizophrenia, secrecy has kept the families from getting help and from avoiding the stigma associated with schizophrenia. Such secrecy has led them to feel isolated from others. The clinician should try to help the families diminish the need for secrecy in their struggle to cope with schizophrenia. The use of the invariant prescription in some ways validates the usefulness of secrecy, a notion I would argue that needs to be discouraged among these families.

Positive Connotations

The technique of using positive connotations helps highlight the change process as a family phenomenon and not an individual phenomenon. When a family member identifies a change in individual behavior as, for example, "Joe seems to be listening better," the therapist relabels this change as a family-level phenomenon, "What you seem to be saying is that you, Joe, and his dad have changed the way you communicate with each other."

For families coping with schizophrenia, this family-level focus can be critical. The family members may feel the focus of therapy must be on getting the person with schizophrenia to change his or her behavior and not appreciate their own roles in creating such opportunities for change. Also, focusing on individual change can increase the expectations and stress level of the person who is the focus of attention. For individuals with schizophrenia this may be an uncomfortable position. An issue such as medication compliance may have to be seen as a family-level phenomenon before change can occur.

Rituals

The final technique is the use of rituals. For a systemic/Milan family therapist, a ritual is a prescribed set of behaviors or tasks that the therapist expects the family to carry out. The outcome of carrying out such behaviors or tasks is to change the overall patterns of behavior and roles within the family. Similar to the directives of strategic family therapy, they are a structured technique for disrupting the status quo within the family. Prior to the more collaborative version of systemic/Milan family therapy, the ritual was developed by the therapist and prescribed for the family based on the therapist's perceived expertise. More recently, such rituals are developed in a more collaborative atmosphere between the therapist and family. The idea of a ritual is present in many types of family therapy, ranging from a very structured technique to a more casual process. For families coping with schizophrenia, collaborating on a new routine or change in roles and behaviors can provide a concrete process for the family to follow. Such concrete steps can help alleviate some of the anxiety and stress experienced by these families.

THE PROCESS OF FAMILY THERAPY

With a family coping with schizophrenia, the process of systemic/Milan family therapy would focus on collaborating with the family in the development of a new sense of themselves as a family system and working toward the disruption of family-level patterns of behavior that inhibit their coping and adaptation in the face of the illness.

Systemic/Milan family therapy is not as structured as strategic or structural family therapy, and much of the process is guided by the use of circular questions. For this reason, the model proceeds best with a fairly verbal family who is willing to engage in the type of discussion necessary to generate the information and hypotheses that guide the process. One of the difficult issues for the family and the family therapist is how to include the person with schizophrenia in this process. The therapist must assess the verbal ability of the person with schizophrenia and determine if the person will be able to function well within this particular model of family therapy.

Collaboration

Provided the person with schizophrenia can participate in a meaningful way in the family therapy, the family could expect some of the following experiences in systemic/Milan family therapy. First, the therapist would present a very collaborative method of working with the family. One of the strengths of the model is its inclusion of the family in establishing the goals and procedures for therapy. Such collaboration was developed further in the growth of solution-focused therapies. The idea is that the family is the expert of its own situation and the therapist takes the stance of needing to learn from the family.

Questions

Such a stance leads to the second experience in systemic/Milan family therapy. The family would be expected to speak extensively about its experiences as a system. The use of questions is pivotal to this model of family therapy. The family could expect the questions to guide it toward a focus on the family system and not on individual issues or pathology. For some families coping with schizophrenia this can be a new experience and a somewhat challenging expectation. Many families get used to the focus being on the person with schizophrenia. Any attempt to shift the focus to the family system can sometimes be interpreted as blaming the family. Again, the issue is not the family system as cause of the schizophrenia, but how the family system promotes or inhibits coping with the illness of schizophrenia. The questions allow the therapist and the family to reflect critically on the family system and develop hypotheses about family functioning.

Insight

Through such hypothesis development and exploration, the family would expect to gain insight into its systemic functioning. Such insight might highlight ingrained patterns of behavior or family games that inhibit the growth and coping of the family. The development of insight would be expected to lead to changes in behavior and communication within the family and between the family members. One of the challenges facing families coping with schizophrenia is the development of insight. This is often expressed as a concern over the lack of insight into the person with schizophrenia. The systemic/Milan family therapist would expand this notion to the level of insight within the family system. Again, some families may experience this as blame. The systemic/Milan family therapist would see it as the first step to uncovering problematic patterns within the family.

Sharing Insight

Finally, the family coping with schizophrenia who participates in systemic/Milan family therapy would expect the therapist to reflect to the family his or her own thoughts about the family. The collaboration between the therapist and family should extend to the sharing of hypotheses, perspectives, and insights gained through the exploration of information gathered by the circular questioning process. Success in therapy would be measured by the extent to which the family moved toward seeing itself as a system and could better respond to the environment and its own individual needs as a system.

Conclusion

What does the future hold for the use of systemic/Milan model of family therapy in working with families coping with schizophrenia? The answer is probably a very limited future. The clinicians and researchers who first developed this model have moved into new territories, including narrative and solution-focused therapies. For this reason, there seems to be a move away from some of the major tenets of this model. Also, some of the early theoretical formulations, including the development of psychosis through family games, run counter to what we now know about schizophrenia. This puts the model on a very weak foundation for working with families coping with schizophrenia. Finally, although the focus on the family as a system is critical, not only to this model but to many models discussed in this book, the approach taken by the systemic/Milan model can come across as blaming the family. The attempt to lessen this perspective through a more collaborative process is well advised. But it may be the case of a good idea coming too late to reverse the sense that this model would be a source of stress for families coping with schizophrenia.

Chapter 9

Cognitive-Behavioral Family Therapy

BRIEF OVERVIEW AND APPLICATION TO SCHIZOPHRENIA

Early Pioneers

Behavior therapy has its origins in the work of the Russian physiologist Ivan Pavlov. Behavioral family therapy owes much of its theoretical base to the work of B. F. Skinner and his ideas on operant conditioning. Cognitive-behavioral family therapy, an outgrowth of these two major theories, has been greatly informed by the work of Albert Ellis and Aaron Beck. These major theorists span the twentieth century. Models of family therapy within the cognitive-behavioral spectrum, which includes behavioral family therapy, cognitive-behavioral family therapy, psychosocial multiple family group therapy, and psychosocial education, all have strong research support and remain very active models in the treatment of schizophrenia. In some studies, cognitive-behavioral spectrum family therapies are seen as the family treatment of choice for working with schizophrenia.

For behavior therapy, the early work of Joseph Wolpe brought ideas from classical conditioning to the treatment of some family and couples issues including sexual dysfunction. However, it was Skinner's operant conditioning that had the greatest impact on behavioral family therapy. Nichols and Schwartz (2001) state, "The operant conditioner carefully observes target behavior and then quantifies its frequency and rate. Then, to complete a functional analysis of the behavior, the experimenter or clinician notes the consequences of the behavior to determine the contingencies of reinforcement" (p. 266). This summary includes a number of theoretical notions that have continued to shape cognitive-behavioral family therapy up to the present. First, the clinical focus is on observable, countable behaviors that the individual or family manifest. Second, the clinician observes for behaviors or transactions that occur that reinforce the manifested behavior. Interventions were then tied to changing or modifying the reinforcements that would then change or modify the target behaviors. Cognitive-behavioral family therapy benefited from such a strong theory development and research base that lent itself well to empirical validation in various clinical settings.

Among some of the practitioners who helped develop cognitive-behavioral theory and practice into a robust model of family therapy are Gerald Patterson, Robert Liberman, Richard Stuart, Ian Falloon, and Neil Jacobson. Both Falloon and Liberman have been instrumental in bringing this model of family therapy to families coping with severe mental illness. In particular, Falloon, Boyd, and McGill (1984) outlined their behavioral family model, which was influential in the development of social skills training and psychoeducational approaches. Likewise, Liberman (1992) brought together a number of cognitive-behavioral clinicians who outlined important advancements in functional assessments, social-skills training, family management, and general psychiatric rehabilitation. More recently, Kim Mueser and Shirley Glynn (1999) provided an extensive overview of this model of family therapy and its use with a variety of mental health conditions.

Consequences

A number of concepts underlie this model of family therapy. As Piercy et al. (1996) point out, the distinction between them is often blurred. The main concept that drives this model is that behavior is driven by consequences. Consequences are reinforcers that help increase or decrease a behavior. Reinforcers that help increase a behavior can be either positive or negative. Punishers are reinforcers that decrease a behavior and include such strategies as aversive control and withdrawing positive reinforcers.

One way consequences can be operationalized within family settings is through the use of a *token economy*. Token economies are also common in some institutional settings that work extensively with the developmentally disabled and people with severe mental illnesses. In a token economy, points or some tangible reward (such as poker chips) are provided as reinforcement once a specified task is completed. In some families coping with schizophrenia, such specific tasks may focus on personal hygiene, medication compliance, or other self-care and interpersonal tasks. As the individual accrues more points or tokens, he or she can then use these to obtain a specific reward. In my experience, families who have tried to implement such a plan find it difficult to identify a reward the individual is willing to work toward (perhaps as a side effect of the anhedonia that can accompany schizophrenia) or they find the individual becomes suspicious over the use of the tokens as a perceived control mechanism (which it actually is). In some cases, battles are waged over the tokens, which then defeats the whole purpose of the plan.

Affect

Affect plays a role within the behavioral family therapy, especially with the growth of cognitive-behavioral therapies. Affect focuses on the subjective experience of feelings and emotions the individual perceives. The cognitive behaviorists see affect as linked to cognitions and to behavior. It becomes imperative to see all three components as inextricably linked together. However, in the illness of schizophrenia, such a linkage is often difficult to discern. Often the person's affect is completely separated from his or her behavior that may, in turn, be completely separated from his or her cognitions. Although it may be useful to try and explore such linkages, it may be a more fruitful search for those individuals who are more stabilized on medication and who can begin to make sense of their affect, thoughts, and behaviors.

Shaping

Shaping is used in behavioral therapies to help an individual learn a new behavior by rewarding the individual when he or she engages in the approximate behavior. As the approximations move closer and closer to the desired behavior, the individual continues to receive rewards as a motivating factor. Often, the term *modeling* is used to describe the process of shaping. However, there is an important distinction. In shaping, the person is working actively to learn a new behavior. In modeling, the person is observing someone else engaging in a behavior and seeing the rewards that person receives for exhibiting the behavior.

Both shaping and modeling can be useful concepts in working with families who are coping with schizophrenia. In residential facilities where I have worked, shaping can be used in the areas of self-care procedures. For individuals experiencing severe and chronic schizophrenia, simple tasks such as brushing teeth or taking a shower may need to be shaped over a course of time. Likewise, modeling can be used by rewarding individuals who attend groups, keep appointments, clean their rooms, and engage in more prosocial type behavior. Within the home, family members become the models who can demonstrate appropriate interpersonal interaction or who can reinforce approximate steps toward a desired behavior such as cleaning a bedroom. However, families often require some guidance in learning how to break down tasks into understandable steps. Also, they need to learn patience as a person with schizophrenia relearns skills and behaviors that the family may take for granted.

Schemas

A final concept that comes more from the cognitive perspective is the idea of schemas. Although schemas are talked about within a variety of theories (e.g., cognitive, psychoanalytic, narrative, and Piagetian), they are basically understood as core beliefs or cognitive templates that a person has that affects how he or she understands and responds to the world. Such core beliefs can be shaped by early life experience or specific and meaningful events in the person's current experience. For a cognitive-behavioral family therapist, assessing for and making explicit such schemas is an important part of the clinical intervention. In working with families coping with schizophrenia, it is not unusual to find family members responding to the individual with schizophrenia based on core beliefs they hold about the nature of the illness and what is expectable of the individual with schizophrenia. Many times, these core beliefs are shaped by a lack of accurate information, misinformation, or fear and reaction to stigma.

ESSENTIAL SKILLS AND TECHNIQUES

Concepts often intermingle with techniques in the behavioral and cognitive-behavioral models of family therapy. Even with this slight level of ambiguity, it is possible to try to isolate a few specific techniques used by these clinicians that may prove useful in working with families coping with schizophrenia.

Contracts

A contract is a written plan that the clinician organizes with the family based on a thorough understanding of the family and the specific problem or goal that is to be dealt with. Often the contract spells out in detail what is expected of each family member, what will happen if a person does not meet expectations, the steps necessary to meet the goal specified, and what types of motivators or rewards are to be utilized to help move individuals and the family as a whole forward. Contracts have the advantage in making the intervention concrete and clear to all involved. It can provide a good gauge for the clinician to determine how well the family is moving forward. However, contracts only work if everyone is agreeable, the steps and expectations are understandable, and the consequences enforceable. I have learned that the two most common errors made in using contracts is to make the steps or expectations too big so that the family feels like a failure from the beginning, and to try and rely on consequences that the family has no way of enforcing.

Coaching

A second technique that is often used is called coaching. In this case, the clinician becomes a hands-on instructor with the family and provides direct advice or suggestions about how to handle a specific interaction. For families coping with schizophrenia, this can be the most important technique a clinician can utilize. Often the family will be at a loss on how to respond to the family member with schizophrenia when he or she is engaging in some kind of symptomatic behavior. In particular, I have found family members particularly troubled by positive symptom behaviors. When the family member with schizophrenia is present in the meetings, whether in a hospital, an office, or in the home, it provides the clinician a here-and-now chance for direct coaching. For example, if the person with schizophrenia is present and begins to talk nonstop and interrupts the other family members, it can be useful to ask, "How do any of you get a word in edgewise when he talks like this?" Sometimes, family members will say, "We don't. We just have to wait until he's through." Such a family may need help in learning how to gently but firmly redirect the conversation and put some appropriate limits on the type or style of conversation initiated by the person with schizophrenia. It is important to remember, however, that each family has its own unique needs and abilities. Clinicians who utilize coaching need to be aware that one technique that works for one family may not be appropriate for others. The suggestions and advice that come from coaching need to be tailored for each family based on a thorough understanding of each one.

Assessment

A final technique, which is actually more a series of techniques or steps, comes under the heading of assessment. One of the strengths of behavioral and cognitive-behavioral interventions is their focus on careful and accurate assessment. Often, such an assessment will be the focus of the first several sessions and may involve the family completing specific homework assignments in order to provide more data. The assessment may try to establish the baseline rate of a specific behavior that is the target for change, or it may involve better delineating the nature of the interactions between specific family members. Behavioral and cognitive-behavioral clinicians have developed a number of checklists and evaluation measures to facilitate careful assessment. In some ways, this sounds similar to Jay Haley's problem stage (see Chapter 8). Both involve careful observation and questioning of the family. Following the assessment, the clinician will use the data to develop a contract specifying the target concern, the steps necessary to change to concerns, the expectations of each family member involved in the process, and a time frame for measuring progress.

THE PROCESS OF FAMILY THERAPY

For families coping with schizophrenia, the process of family therapy from a behavioral or cognitive-behavioral perspective can be very reassuring. In many of the families I have talked to over the years, they have generally perceived these models as providing the quickest and most concrete feedback for their specific concerns. Although other models may be perceived as filled with a lot of talking, these models are seen as more action-oriented.

Assessment

In general, most families could expect to go through a thorough assessment at the onset of clinical services. Here, however, is the first place things can begin to go wrong in the clinical process. Many families who have been stressed out or overburdened by caring for someone with schizophrenia may see the assessment as a chance to focus on only the troubling behavior of the person with schizophrenia. It can sometimes take on the appearance of a "fix my son/daughter and we will all be happy" session. Although such a reaction is understandable, the family clinician has to walk a fine line between responding to the family's level of stress and looking at the family as a whole. As mentioned before, the person with schizophrenia may feel left out of the process or feel as though he or she has no voice in the family, no voice to speak up about troubling interactions he or she perceives coming from other members of the family. The family clinician needs to pay careful attention to including the person with schizophrenia in the assessment process.

Contracts

Once the assessment is completed or near completion, a contract will be developed with the family. As previously discussed, the contract will specify the goals and objectives of service and the expectations of each person involved. Here again, it is important that the specified goals be ones the entire family can agree on and get behind. If it is perceived that only one person in the family is setting the agenda, it is unlikely the rest of the family will cooperate fully with the clinical process. This includes the person with schizophrenia.

Homework Assignments

Once the contract is developed, the family will begin regular meetings to focus on the goals of the contract and how each person is fulfilling his or her expectations. Often, the family clinician may use specific homework assignments to move the process along. Homework assignments are often assigned tasks the family (or some subset of the family) is expected to carry out between sessions with the clinician (such as the whole family getting together to do something fun or obtaining an application for a rehabilitation program). Some families may be asked to read something (in particular, information about schizophrenia that may challenge some of their core beliefs). It is important that the homework assignments connect logically to the goals spelled out in the contract and that the family is aware of this connection. One of the most common reasons families fail to complete a homework assignment is that they fail to see how it moves them forward toward their goals.

Role of the Clinician

Unlike other models of family intervention, many behavioral or cognitive-behavioral clinicians will be very active in the sessions. Through coaching, shaping, modeling, information sharing, and specific skill training exercises, the clinician has a large repertoire available to provide immediate feedback and response to family concerns. For some families, this can be a strange experience. It is useful for the family clinician to orient the family to how the intervention may go so that the possible level of activity does not take the family aback within each session. Such activity should be sensitive to what the person with schizophrenia can handle. For example, hands-on experiential coaching in the session can be very helpful but only if the person with schizophrenia, if he or she is expected to be involved, is not too symptomatic to participate. Otherwise, the experience may fail and reinforce the core beliefs of the family that they are incapable of change and/or that the person with schizophrenia is incapable of change.

Termination

With the use of a contract, it is easier to track progress toward the goals. For this reason, termination of intervention is usually tied to a percentage of success in achieving the specified goals. As the family and clinician review progress, the family will have a clear idea of where it is and how much longer services are likely to be available. Although termination should not be a surprise, it still needs to be dealt with as a major transition and potential loss of support for the family. This includes being sensitive to the person with schizophrenia and how he or she may feel about termination.

Conclusion

What does the future hold for the use of behavioral/cognitive-behavioral models of family therapy in working with families coping with schizophrenia? The answer is probably very positive but with one or two caveats. As Nichols and Schwartz (2001) state, "Behavior therapy was born and bred in a tradition of research, and it's not surprising that behavioral family therapy is the most carefully studied form of family treatment" (p. 295). Such a statement could also be made about its use with families coping with schizophrenia. The strength of the model shows in how it has influenced other models such as psychoeducational and multifamily group treatment. It is one model that continues to be used not just for schizophrenia but also for a whole host of major psychiatric difficulties.

Now, however, come the caveats. First, many studies using behavioral interventions demonstrate its efficacy (how well it performs under controlled conditions), but not its effectiveness (how well it performs under normal conditions such as in a clinic or hospital ward). More research on effectiveness is needed. Second, behavioral models often follow a linear way of thinking. One person's behavior causes a response or reaction in another person. Such linear thinking is contradictory to the systems and circular causality thinking of most family clinicians. Third, many families coping with schizophrenia are struggling with multiple problems within multiple-systems levels in their lives. Behavioral models can come across as overly simplistic and reductionistic for these families. Finally, given that many families are stressed out from trying to cope with schizophrenia, it is easy for this model to place the focus squarely on the person with schizophrenia and expect that person to be the only one required to change. Again, this linear and overly reductionistic view may be counterproductive for many families.

With those caveats in place, these models will continue to be utilized in the family intervention with schizophrenia. As more effectiveness studies occur, the models will be refined to increase their usefulness for these families. It is also reasonable to expect that clinicians working within other models will adopt many of the techniques developed through these models. That is certainly a vote of confidence about the strength and utility of these models.

Chapter 10

Narrative Family Therapy

BRIEF OVERVIEW AND APPLICATION TO SCHIZOPHRENIA

Early Pioneers

Narrative family therapy has its base in the philosophical writings of Michel Foucault, a prominent French intellectual whose work greatly influenced a number of fields and professions, and Jerome Bruner's work on culture and language. In addition, a number of writers from the fields of anthropology, sociology, and the history of science all touched on issues related to the development of narrative theory. Individuals such as Gregory Bateson, Clifford Geertz, Sander Gilman, Karl Tomm, Kenneth Gergen, and the "symbolic interactionist" school of sociology have all played a part. Within the field of family therapy, there is an umbrella term used, *social constructionist,* which tries to incorporate many types of practitioners who have been influenced by these writers. However, the focus of this chapter will be on the family therapists who fit more specifically within the narrative part of social constructionist practice. Chapter 11 will focus more on those family therapists that fit within the solution-focused part of social constructionist practice.

Narrative therapy emerged in the late 1970s through the work and writing of Michael White, a social worker who lives in Australia. Along with his colleagues David Epston and Cheryl White, they began to articulate a view of narrative theory that built on some original ideas of Gregory Bateson and Michel Foucault. In particular, issues related to how people think about and construct a view of their world and the role discourse plays in such constructions figured prominently in their writings. Two books co-authored by White and Epston (White and Epston, 1990; Epston and White, 1992) have formed the foundation for narrative therapy. In addition, Zimmerman and Dickerson (1996) wrote a very user-friendly guide to narrative therapy. Although very few of these writers have focused exclusively on schizophrenia within the family context, my own writing (Marley, 1999) has begun to try to translate this model into direct practice for this population. This theory and model are still relatively new, but some of the key concepts that structure the approach have been discussed for many years.

Dominant Beliefs

The most important concept within narrative theory is that what we perceive around us is shaped by the dominant beliefs that shape what we see and how we think about what we see. Since each person may be shaped differently by cultural beliefs, each person may construct reality in an individual or idiosyncratic manner. Narrative theory embraces the notion of multiple realities, that each person will perceive the world differently. In narrative family therapy, then, the goal is not to find the one truth under which every member of the family operates, but to discover the multiple truths at work within each family and within each family member. For some this is an idea that can empower a family and lend credence to each member's perspective. For others, this notion supports ambiguity and a lack of any real solid foundation, a single reality, upon which to build.

The most obvious examples of dominant cultural beliefs for the purposes of this book are the notions of *family* and *schizophrenia*. The concept of family is directly influenced by what our history and culture tell us about families. In a sense, our schema or core beliefs, shaped by history and culture, influence what we perceive. If the dominant narrative of our society is that a family must have a mother, a father, and their biological children, then any family not fitting within that narrative expectation (e.g., single-parent families, gay and lesbian families) will be viewed as pathological by clinicians who hold to the dominant narrative. For Foucault, one of the primary questions posed by this kind of thinking is, What force determines the dominant narrative? Who shapes the culture that places all human interaction into a specific context? Foucault used the metaphor of archeology to describe his work in historical analysis that allowed him to uncover some of the key people and processes that gave rise to dominant narratives. Likewise, a family therapist must function as an archeologist to uncover how a family has come to see itself and its members within a particular narrative construction (Marley, 1999). What a family tells itself about itself will greatly impact what the family can do with itself.

The diagnostic term schizophrenia is also susceptible to narrative shaping and distortion. Foucault (1965) and Gilman (1985) have explored historical influences on both our perceptions of people with severe mental illnesses and on the processes of diagnosis and treatment. Not surprisingly, these authors found many examples of how dominant cultural narratives directly shaped how people with mental illness were represented to the broader public and how such presentations shaped the treatments made available. Some of this historical influence (or baggage as the case may be) is still felt today every time the media misrepresents the illness of schizophrenia as one of split personality.

Discourse

For the narrative family therapist, discourse exists at two levels. First there is the cultural discourse that shapes the perception of reality and how such perceptions influence the structure and the function of the family. Second, there is the discourse created within each family that follows the same "rule" as the level-one discourse, which is those in the family who have the power often shape the discourse. For the family therapist, then, one of the keys is to help the family articulate these narratives that exist on both levels, bring them out for scrutiny, and help the family determine if the narratives are helping or hindering them in some aspect of its existence.

Within a family living with schizophrenia, the level-two discourse may be about the illness itself. In some of my clinical work (Marley, 1992, 1999), I have found family members often engage in discourse that seeks to control or disempower the person with schizophrenia. Sometimes this is accomplished on a covert level, sometimes it is more overt. Other discourse may reinforce the notion that the illness and the person with the illness are the only problems influencing the family. In a sense, if you fix or cure the illness, you will fix the family.

Unfortunately, one discourse many families still contend with is the historical notion of family blame for the illness of schizophrenia. Often this is made overt in family sessions when one parent accuses the other of some parenting lapse that seems to coincide with the beginning of symptoms in the person with schizophrenia.

Externalization

A final concept found in narrative family therapy is the idea of externalization. This concept also figures prominently in some of the brief and solution-focused models discussed in Chapter 11. Externalization involves helping the family see the problem or issue as residing outside of a specific individual. It prevents the development of an identified patient, someone who is in possession of the problem, by making the problem an almost tangible entity that descends upon the family as a whole. Throughout this book, for example, I have tried to use the phrases "the family living with schizophrenia" or "the family coping with schizophrenia" as examples of externalization. Although clearly one person in the family may carry the specific diagnosis, it is an issue that resides within and must be dealt with by the entire family. As with strategic family therapy, the power of language is nurtured in narrative family therapy. Externalization, the use of metaphor, and the careful exploration and articulation of family discourse all rely on the power of language.

ESSENTIAL SKILLS AND TECHNIQUES

Questions

The importance of language in narrative family therapy is made explicit in the model by the focus on careful questioning. As with strategic and solution-focused family therapy, much of the technique or art of the model resides in the careful use of specific types of questions. In my clinical writing on narrative family therapy with schizophrenia (Marley, 1999), I outlined a number of types of questions that can be used for different reasons. It is through these various types of questions that the family's narrative can emerge. Some of the types of questions include strengths questions (e.g., What's going fine for all of you right now?), discourse questions (e.g., How does this belief influence you and your family?), and change questions (e.g., What does the family need to believe if change is going to happen?).

Externalization

Externalization was previously mentioned as an underlying concept. But it also exists as a technique. Again, through the use of questions or in the process of exploring and articulating discourse, the clinician tries to keep the process of externalization active throughout the session. With families living with schizophrenia, the illness of schizophrenia can be seen as an internal problem of one individual that has consequences for all family members. The process and technique of externalization tries to reconfigure how the family sees the illness and the person with the illness. Rather than focus on the individual with schizophrenia, the clinician may say, "When schizophrenia came into your family, how did it affect everyone?" The illness becomes similar to an overbearing relative who comes for a visit uninvited and who then stays too long. Although such a perspective is not meant to diminish the impact of the illness on the person with schizophrenia, it frees up the family to look at the illness' impact on the larger family system. This has the potential result of moving away from blaming the individual (or blaming the parents) for the illness.

Storytelling

The various types of questions used in narrative family therapy are aimed at helping the family articulate its story. The process of creating stories, both the family story and each person's individualized story, becomes the main focus of the therapy. The clinician can use the idea and technique of storytelling as a concrete event in the therapy. It is crucial, however, to prepare and orient the family for such a process. Some families may not see the point of storytelling if they are expecting concrete answers to their questions about coping with schizophrenia. The clinician needs to lay the groundwork early in the therapy to help the family understand how the stories we tell ourselves about our family and our problems affect how we interact with one another and try to solve our problems. If the family can see this as a real issue, the family members will be more open to storytelling.

Letters

One last technique used by narrative family therapy clinicians is the use of letters. White and Epston (1990) discuss the use of letters in detail. The letter is a logical outgrowth of the concept of discourse and family narrative. The clinician can use the letter as a way of extending the reach of the session by reminding a family of the issues discussed, how the narrative is being constructed, reinforce the process of externalization, raise new questions for the family to contemplate prior to the next session, and to reinforce the family's progress to date. For families living with schizophrenia, I have found their reactions to my letters to be very positive. They indicated they appreciated the positive comments and could sometimes better "hear" my take on what was going on in the privacy of a letter than in the actual session. I also encourage family members to write letters to each other, but not as a substitute for talking during a session. For some families for whom weekly sessions may be a burden or not required, the use of letters also can extend the connection between family and clinician between scheduled meetings.

THE PROCESS OF FAMILY THERAPY

A family living with schizophrenia that seeks out a family therapist who works within the narrative model should expect to have a very collaborative experience. Narrative therapy is infused with the idea of social justice, in particular the ideas that the family is the author and expert of its own situation and that each family member's perception of the family's reality needs to be heard and respected. This creates a different experience for families than if they were exposed to some of the other models outlined in this book. For the family living with schizophrenia, the respect they feel and the expertise they are encouraged to embrace can be refreshing.

Questions

The basic process of narrative family therapy is the use of questions. The clinician utilizes the various types of questions to help the family construct its story, its narrative, about how and why the family feels, thinks, and functions the way that it does. In my work with families coping with schizophrenia (Marley, 1999), I indicated that the clinician functions as an "investigative archeologist" and stated that "information gathered through such questioning becomes the starting point for challenging the family's pathology discourse, developing material to use in setting goals and objectives, and creating a more positive environment" (p. 6). For the clinician working with families living with schizophrenia, it is vital that the individual with schizophrenia be an active member in this process. Obviously, depending on the degree of severity of the symptoms, the clinician and the family may have to adjust their expectations of the individual with schizophrenia for involvement or ability to contribute to the discussion. But even if the person's ability to participate is minimal, that participation needs to be supported and respected.

Deconstruction

Once the family narrative is constructed and made explicit, the family and the clinician can begin to examine and deconstruct the narrative. Such examination tries to assist the family in seeing how the particular narrative shapes the family's behavior and how it tries to deal with the problems associated with the illness of schizophrenia. Deconstruction involves taking apart the narrative and searching for erroneous assumptions, power struggles, and faulty logic that underlie some parts of the narrative. Through this process the family can begin to identify parts of the narrative that do not serve the family's best interest and begin to think of alternative narratives that might better suit the family's needs.

Construction

The process of creation or construction follows deconstruction. The family is encouraged to collaborate on the construction of a new narrative that builds on its identified strengths and gives voice to the particular needs and strengths of each individual. For families living with schizophrenia, this can be particularly helpful. Many families are so caught up in the single focus of the presence of pathology in one of its members that they lose sight of the family as a whole and its needs and strengths. The new narrative becomes the new schema that is used to reinterpret the presence of schizophrenia in the family, how the family can cope, and where the family can grow in the future. The family establishes a new meaning that incorporates the presence of schizophrenia, but does not perseverate on this one facet.

Conclusion

What does the future hold for the use of narrative therapy for families living with schizophrenia? I would hope the future looks bright. The concepts that underlie narrative theory seem very relevant to working with this population. In particular the idea of social justice and the need to understand how the larger culture can influence the family and how it understands and copes with schizophrenia are very germane in the face of continued stigma, family blame, and disempowerment by some parts of the medical/psychiatric community.

However, more needs to be done to test out how well the various concepts and techniques work with these families. Currently, few clinicians who work with these families seem to use this model. Also, as with so many of the models discussed in this book, there is a lack of research demonstrating the efficacy and effectiveness of this model. This is still a relatively new model, so perhaps much of this developmental work is still to come.

Chapter 11

Solution-Focused Family Therapy

BRIEF OVERVIEW AND APPLICATION TO SCHIZOPHRENIA

Early Pioneers

Somewhat concurrently with the development of narrative therapy, another model of family therapy was taking shape. Directly influenced by the work of the family therapy pioneer Jay Haley and the work of Haley's guide, Milton Erickson, as well as grounded in some of the ideas of social constructivist theory, solution-focused family therapy emerged on the scene as a somewhat radical departure from more traditional models of family therapy. It is interesting to note that two excellent books on family therapy, Nichols and Schwartz (2001) and Piercy et al. (1996), position solution-focused therapy in slightly different ways. Nichols and Schwartz see it as a logical outgrowth of the Mental Research Institute (MRI), strategic, and Milan models and place it with these in one chapter. Piercy et al. place it in the social constructivist chapter alongside narrative family therapy. This somewhat eclectic background speaks to some of the potential strengths of the model as well as some of its weaknesses.

For the most part, solution-focused family therapy was developed at the Brief Family Therapy Center in Milwaukee, Wisconsin. At the end of the 1970s and the beginning of the 1980s, a group of clinicians, primarily led by Steve de Shazer, formed the center. de Shazer had been influenced by the MRI model and spent some time working at Palo Alto. Through the late 1980s and early 1990s, he authored a number of very influential books that articulated the basic tenets of the solution-focused process (de Shazer, 1985, 1991, 1994). Other key figures in the development of solution-focused family therapy include Insoo Berg, Michele Weiner-Davis, Scott Miller, Bill O'Hanlon, John Walter, and Jane Peller. Most are active writers and frequent presenters at family therapy conferences around the country. Unfortunately, almost none of these clinicians included discussions of or work with families living with schizophrenia. The model has been utilized in the treatment of addiction, certainly a potentially severe condition, and has been found useful. It was not until Rowan and O'Hanlon (1999) presented their book focusing on chronic and severe mental illness that the basic theory and techniques of solution-focused therapy could be seen against this specific backdrop.

Focus on the Present

The main concepts of solution-focused family therapy stem from the basic notion that people really do want to change but are limited by their negative views of their problems. Similar to the narrative model's idea of a pathological discourse, solution-focused work tries to help the family members talk differently about their issues and arrive at a different sense of their own reality. The concepts and techniques of solution-focused therapy help facilitate this search for a different way of talking. Another basic notion held by most solution-focused clinicians is the idea that the past is of little consequence in trying to solve the current dilemma. Similar to the strategic model, there is very little focus on background issues or family history. The model focuses very much on the here and now and what families can do today to change the way they think and feel about their present concern.

Exceptions

Out of this focus on the present and on the need to create a new language about the family situation come a number of concepts that try to further this process. A key concept in solution-focused work is the existence of exceptions. An exception is a time when the family is not engaging in the identified problem or has found some way to temporarily solve the problem. Most solution-focused clinicians will zero in on these exception times and try to help the family identify what made the situation better. By bringing attention to such exceptions, the clinician can also challenge the family's belief that the problem is intractable. For example, in a family living with schizophrenia, the family may focus on medication compliance as a constant source of stress. In asking the family if this is always the case, the family may indicate some days when compliance is not a concern. The clinician may follow up with additional questions meant to clarify what went well on those days that led, at least in part, to a solution to the concern. By digging for more details, the clinician can help the family identify strategies it has already hit upon that may move toward a better resolution of the problem.

Dominant Narrative

A second major concept connects solution-focused work with narrative therapy. Both models build on the idea of a dominant narrative that shapes the family's perception of the problem. Such a narrative can drive the family to see problems in a limited way or act in a limited way. Both models try to help the family identify such a dominant narrative and seek out new narratives that may help the family expand its possibilities in how it sees the problem or can cope with the problem. For families coping with schizophrenia, many of these dominant narratives tend to focus on the illness of schizophrenia and what it is doing to the ill individuals and the family as a whole. If the narrative reinforces the belief that "Our family would be great if it wasn't for this illness," the family will often blame the ill individual for all of the family's problems and expect the only change to occur within the person with schizophrenia.

Language

A final major concept of the model focuses on the power of language. As with narrative therapy, the creation of language through conversations between the family and the therapist, and the language the family brings with it to the therapy, provide the main ingredients for both the articulation of the main narrative and the construction of a new narrative. Similar to narrative, strategic, and systemic models, there is a primary focus on the use of questions to help develop the level of conversation necessary for the work to be done. Unfortunately, the "language-heavy" sense of solution-focused work may raise some concerns when working with a family coping with schizophrenia. Because none of the theoreticians behind the development of solution-focused therapy worked with schizophrenia, it is difficult to tell how they would integrate a person with an illness that can affect how the person speaks about and comprehends the world. The danger is that those who have the best ability to speak about the situation (i.e., the other family members) may dominate the session, thus adding to the sense of disempowerment and isolation the person with schizophrenia may already feel. In a sense, the person the clinician most wants to hear from may have the least ability to speak.

General and Specific Principles

Rowan and O'Hanlon (1999) outline five general principles and seven specific principles in their application of solution-focused work with people with schizophrenia.

1. Don't get hooked by the hopelessness of the situation.
2. For the moment, discard diagnoses and relate to your client.
3. Beware of others' evaluations.
4. Cultivate a "beginner's mind."
5. Remember that these clients can and do change. (p. 141)

The general principles focus on maintaining hope, building a relationship with the client, and believing change is possible. The specific principles include:

1. Determine the "customer" for therapy.
2. Acknowledge your clients' point of view.
3. Ask what the person or the family wants.
4. Find out the person's strengths.
5. Think small.
6. Separate the problem from the person.
7. Do inclusive inner work to calm and value the person. (pp. 142-145)

These principles seem to fit nicely with the overall concepts and techniques of the solution-focused approach.

ESSENTIAL SKILLS AND TECHNIQUES

Compliments

Many of the techniques outlined by various practitioners of solution-focused models focus on developing conversation and seeking out exceptions. As one way of developing the conversation between family and therapist, the therapist can use compliments to further the therapeutic relationship and the ability to generate useful dialogue. Compliments are given to the family throughout the session to help diminish anxiety, point out steps the family has already taken to resolve its concerns, and establish a sense of hope within the family. For families coping with schizophrenia, such reassurances are very welcome and empowering.

Questions

A second major technique is the use of questions. Solution-focused clinicians have a number of specific types of questions available to help the family identify exceptions or begin to think differently about its situation. Some of the types of questions include the miracle question, scaling questions, exception-finding questions, coping questions, and "what's better?" questions.

De Jong and Miller (1995) provide a very cogent analysis of many of these types of questions. The most famous of these types of questions is the *miracle question.* It is usually phrased as "Suppose you went to bed last night and while you slept a miracle happened and your problem disappeared. How would you know this occurred when you woke up the next morning?" Such a question forces the family to identify markers that indicate the presence or absence of the problem.

Scaling questions not only help the family put its concerns in perspective but also forces it to think about exceptions. A scaling question usually takes the form of "On a scale of 1 to 10 (1 being a great concern and 10 being no concern), how concerned are you about this problem?" If the family answers that it is about a 3, the clinician can seek out reasons why it is not a 1 or a 2 and how the family can make it a 5 or a 6. In some families coping with schizophrenia, there may be concern about how well the person with schizophrenia can get along in family get-togethers. Such a family might be asked how worried it is that the family will have a good time at the mother's next birthday party. If the family indicates it is a level 3 concern, the family can be asked what prevents it from being a level 1 (thus identifying some current positives or strengths) and how the family can make it at least a level 6 or 7 by the time of the party (thus identifying positive steps the family can take to resolve the concern).

Tasks

A final technique used in solution-focused therapy is the use of tasks. This is similar to the use of tasks in the strategic model previously discussed. Two specific types of tasks most often discussed in this model are the *formula first-session task* and the *more-of-the-same task.* The formula first-session task occurs, obviously enough, at the end of the first session. The family is asked to think about what they do not want to change about their current situation. This forces the family to contemplate its strengths and shift its thinking away from a strictly problem-centered narrative. The more-of-the-same task arises once an exception is identified. If family members can identify a time when the problem seemed resolved, they are asked to try and duplicate the events or environment that led to the resolution. In a sense, the family is asked to do more of what seemed to work.

Elsewhere (Marley, 1992), I discussed a case in which the family found it easiest to interact positively with their son who has schizophrenia when the whole family went bowling. Using that as an exception, the family was encouraged to find more time to work bowling into its routine. For many families living with schizophrenia, the focus on the problems interferes with the ability to remember to make exceptions. It is often very easy to identify such exceptions once the family feels comfortable and can begin to relate to the clinician.

THE PROCESS OF FAMILY THERAPY

A family living with schizophrenia that receives services from a clinician using the solution-focused approach could expect the sessions to focus almost exclusively on the current family functioning. In keeping with the basic tenets of the model, very little emphasis is placed on searching for historical information about the family and its members. The family could also expect a very active clinician who would ask the family numerous questions to help them focus on the current situation and steps the family has taken to try and resolve the current problem.

As with the strategic model, the clinician usually tries to help the family focus on one issue that is affecting the current family experience. Once that issue is articulated, the clinician will ask the family questions centered on that concern and how the family has tried to resolve it. Compared to some other models, solution-focused clinicians tend to be very active in sessions, asking lots of questions, giving compliments, and trying to help the family focus and externalize the current concern. If the family is not used to such an active clinician, they may be a little put off by the unexpected activity.

For families living with schizophrenia, the level of activity may cause some concern. Some families may worry that the activity level will be too much for the person with schizophrenia or that the constant questions and dialogue may make it difficult for the person with schizophrenia to join in. Since each person with schizophrenia is different, the clinician and the family will have to monitor the experience to ensure it is not overwhelming for the individual.

The family can expect much of the focus to be on its strengths and resources. Again, for some families who are expecting to talk only about their problems, this shift can be unexpected. A family coping with schizophrenia may be so used to mental health professionals' exclusive focus on the illness of schizophrenia that the family may find it difficult to think about strengths and resources. I found it helpful to assist the family members in defining what they think strengths and resources are and then asking questions to help them identify what in their life constitutes a strength or a resource. Often the definitions vary by family and even within a family.

The solution-focused clinician should try to help the family see the connection between the focus on the present, finding what has worked, and the focus on strengths as building a pathway toward seeing and thinking differently about the family and its concerns. As with the narrative family therapy model, the solution-focused model ultimately wants to assist the family in seeing the world differently, in a more hopeful and empowered manner. The family can take this new perspective forward into helping itself deal with the current concern and future concerns.

Conclusion

What does the future hold for the solution-focused approach as it applies to working with families with schizophrenia? It would seem the future looks good, but perhaps not in the model's current form. Although the focus on solutions and strengths is extremely important, the model may be too simplistic to help families coping with schizophrenia that may be experiencing numerous concerns simultaneously. Families who are stressed out, depleted of resources, struggling financially, coping with stigma, and trying to manage day to day with a relative with schizophrenia may have difficulty finding assistance with this model. Most families would certainly benefit from some aspects of solution-focused therapy, and these aspects certainly show up in other models discussed throughout this book. In fact, one of the concerns sometimes expressed about the solution-focused model is that it is mostly good clinical work, some aspects of which were articulated in the past by people such as Carl Rogers. In a sense, we have come full circle from the 1950s and 1960s back to the present and are still talking about the same concepts and techniques.

The model has not been used consistently with families coping with schizophrenia. More work needs to be done, both clinical development and research, to better determine how it works with this population and what it has to offer that may be unique. The model certainly has much to offer and it is expected it will be around for some time to come.

Chapter 12

Multiple Family Group Therapy

BRIEF OVERVIEW AND APPLICATION TO SCHIZOPHRENIA

Early Pioneers

Multiple family group therapy (MFGT) developed in the early 1960s as a way of trying to control patient-management problems on psychiatric wards. The early work of Detre et al. (1961) and Laqueur, LaBurt, and Morong (1964) helped establish the theoretical and practical aspects of this mode of intervention. McFarlane has continued to develop this model and helped merge some aspects of MFGT with psychoeducational approaches (McFarlane, 1983, 1990, 1995; McFarlane and Cunningham, 1996).

Overview

MFGT attempts to work with several families at once in a large group format. The family group is led by clinicians, usually at least two, who try to guide the families to discuss their issues, get feedback from the other families, and utilize the group as a problem-solving resource and a help in developing a larger social network. In many cases, the groups are illness-specific, such as a group only for families who have a member with schizophrenia. Unlike some of the models of psychoeducation previously discussed, in MFGT the individual family member with schizophrenia is present in the sessions.

Application to Schizophrenia

Over the past four decades, MFGT has been discussed at length in clinical literature and has been well researched. MFGT was developed through work with the severely mentally ill, primarily people with schizophrenia. The basic theoretical assumptions, goals, and techniques have all been developed and tested with this population. Unlike other models of family therapy that began with this population but then moved on to less severely ill populations, MFGT has remained, in general, an active form of intervention in the treatment of schizophrenia. William McFarlane has remained one of the major contributors to the growth and continued utilization of MFGT.

ESSENTIAL SKILLS AND TECHNIQUES

Goals of MFGT

McFarlane (1983) presents the best outline of the basic goals, types, and phases of MFGT. The three main goals of MFGT are the prevention of relapse, the improvement of psychosocial functioning, and the expansion of the family's social network. Prevention of relapse focuses on the reduction of isolation, the reduction of stigma and burden, reduction of expressed emotion in the family, and reduction of overall communication dysfunction in the family. Improved psychosocial functioning focuses on correcting or eliminating any dependency-inducing interactions among the family members. Social network expansion focuses on the creation of a semipermanent social network organized around the long-term needs of the families with members with schizophrenia.

Types of MFGT

There are four basic types of MFGT structures, each of which has a corresponding degree of effectiveness. The first type of MFGT is the short-term duration group with an open membership. Open membership implies that new families can join the group at any point in time. McFarlane believed this to be the least-effective type of MFGT. The second type of MFGT is the short-term duration group with a closed membership. Closed membership implies that no new families can join the group once it is formed and meeting. McFarlane viewed this type as being somewhat more effective than the first type. The third type of MFGT is the long-term duration group with an open membership. McFarlane judged this type to be more effective than the second. The fourth type of MFGT is the long-term duration group with a closed membership. McFarlane believed this to be the most effective type of MFGT.

Phases of MFGT

McFarlane's model of MFGT has four phases. Most of the skills and techniques required to effectively run a MFGT come out of trying to manage the group process as it moves through these phases. Clinicians who run MFGT sessions need to be familiar with not only family dynamics but also group dynamics. The first phase in MFGT is *assembling the group.* At this phase the clinician tries to gather information about each family member and assess the degree to which they could participate in the therapy. Two elements of this assessment are to explore the family's understanding of the illness and what goals the family has for its involvement. In addition, the clinician needs to estimate each family member's strengths and weaknesses and how each might function in the group. Finally, the clinician must explain in detail the goals and process of MFGT and the role of the clinician leading the group.

Upon gathering this information and forming impressions about each family, the clinician must then assemble the group. McFarlane suggests four elements that go into making a successful group. First, the group should be homogeneous as to the diagnosis. Second, the group should be heterogeneous as to family style, class, and ethnicity. Third, there are some advantages to grouping by age. Each MFG should feature families at about the same age and developmental level, such as families with adolescents who are mentally ill or families coping with an older member who is mentally ill. Fourth, the optimal group size seems to be between four and seven families. This number provides sufficient diversity and group dynamics without overwhelming either each family or the clinician.

The second phase of MFGT is *building group cohesion.* This is accomplished by a number of group dynamic processes and specific techniques utilized by the clinician. First, group members get a chance to introduce themselves to everyone. Often, this is accompanied by some comment about what is going on in the family. Second, if the membership is open, the group members who have been there the longest can help orient the newer families to the MFGT process. Third, throughout the provision of the MFGT, the clinician attempts to keep the conversation going between families, as opposed to directed at the clinician. The clinician can accomplish this by reframing questions, directing family members to respond to a family member's question, or encouraging different families to talk to each other. Fourth, the clinician tries to establish a tone in the group by indicating the inherent expertise of each family in its knowledge of its particular situation and attempts at coping. Families can utilize each other as resident experts in managing the day-to-day events and stresses of living with someone with schizophrenia. As the group progresses, such activity helps develop a sense of group cohesion. This cohesion is essential in developing a sense of trust and safety for the group members. Trust and safety are crucial to accomplishing the next goal.

The third phase of MFGT is *disenmeshment* and *problem solving.* Group cohesion allows the families to discuss, question, and confront one another about each family's specific dynamics, beliefs, and communication styles. Family members are encouraged to use the group as a problem-solving resource as individual family members, or the entire family, seek to resolve long-standing issues or crisis situations. Disenmeshment applies to family boundaries and internal family relationships. The group can often be helpful in pointing out how family boundaries or relationship styles directly affect the family's ability to cope with schizophrenia.

The fourth phase of MFGT, which in actuality has been occurring throughout the process, is *building a social support network.* One outcome of a successful MFGT is the establishment of new connections and resources that may continue outside of the group. The experience of seeing other families struggling to cope with schizophrenia, of seeing other people experience some of the same emotions, and of seeing people from all walks of life trying to cope with schizophrenia can alleviate much of the sense of isolation experienced by families coping with schizophrenia.

THE PROCESS OF FAMILY THERAPY

The four phases of MFGT are facilitated by some of the following processes. However, since the setting in which MFGT occurs can affect how the MFGT proceeds, clinicians may have to modify their groups to meet the specific needs of their population. In many inpatient settings, MFGT has an open-membership policy due to the turnover experienced in the setting. In outpatient settings, closed-membership groups are more possible. Once the clinicians assemble the group, the MFGT can begin. Assuming some degree of group cohesion has been established, there are a number of processes that can take place to move the MFGT along.

The Greek Chorus

One process often used in MFGT is the "single-family focus" experience, or what I like to call "the Greek chorus." One family is selected, perhaps because they are having more difficulty or are struggling with an issue that resonates with many of the other families. The selected family (if they agree to go along) is placed facing each other in the center of the larger circle. The MFGT leader may give the family a topic or situation to discuss or a problem to solve that is related to the family's specific needs. As the family begins to process the activity, the other families, the Greek chorus, can provide feedback, commentary, and concrete suggestions or guidance to help the family along. Often, in the process of focusing on and helping a single family, the other families bring up issues or ideas that are relevant to their own experience. For families living with schizophrenia, the MFGT leader needs to be attentive to how much stress the family can handle before suggesting they take center stage. The intense focus can be overwhelming for some families.

The Family Leader

Another tool used in MFGT is the family leader. Building on the notion of empowerment and connection, the MFGT leader asks that a specific family take over some of the leadership roles for a particular meeting or a series of meetings. This shared leadership can be rotated among different families at regular time intervals. The group leader will have to be in tune with the families to know which family may be under too much stress or too anxious to take on such a role.

Other Processes

Other techniques a clinician can use come from the area of group therapy. The clinician may have the group or some element of the group role-play specific situations and then receive feedback from the rest of the group. Individual families may request specific time to focus on an issue that they are struggling with and need group support and feedback to help resolve. In many MFGT sessions, especially in an inpatient setting, the issue of discharge and follow-up care are important topics. With an open membership, this topic has a tendency to come up repeatedly. However, it can be important and powerful for families who are new to the group to hear how other families think through and resolve issues around discharge and follow-up.

More recently, McFarlane (2002) and others have worked to combine the essential features of the traditional MFGT with the structure of traditional psychoeducational models. The Multiple Family Group Psychoeducation Model is a strong integration of the strengths of these two models. The model follows some of the same components of the traditional MFGT, specifically joining with families, building a social network or families, and helping families develop problem-solving skills. The incorporation of psychoeducational components, primarily educating families about schizophrenia, helps facilitate some of the goals of the traditional MFGT process.

Conclusion

What does the future hold for multiple family group therapy and its second-generation developments? It is clear the future is very bright for these models. The continued use, strong research support, and demonstrated effectiveness in meeting the needs of families living with schizophrenia shows a robust model in need of better dissemination throughout the mental-health services community. This model is an ideal starting place for agencies and clinicians looking to develop some family-oriented programming for families living with schizophrenia. I hope more clinicians become familiar with the concepts and techniques of this model and make it available to more of their clientele.

Chapter 13

The Psychoeducational Model

BRIEF OVERVIEW AND APPLICATION TO SCHIZOPHRENIA

Overview

Unlike some of the models of family intervention discussed in this book, the psychoeducational model was developed directly from work with families coping with schizophrenia. The model was developed in reaction to some of the theories on the etiology of schizophrenia. As previously mentioned, at one time families were blamed for the development of schizophrenia. Later, when these theories lost their credibility, the focus shifted to seeing families as contributing to the environment within which the person with schizophrenia lives.

One model that tried to articulate this view, the *diathesis stress theory,* indicated that a person is born predisposed to the biological illness of schizophrenia but must be in a certain type of environment for that predisposition to express itself. As research continued on the neurobiology of schizophrenia, the focus shifted again away from seeing the family as contributing to the expression of schizophrenia and toward seeing the family environment as playing a key role in the course of the illness. Certain types of family environments, it was thought, could contribute to the relapse potential of a person with schizophrenia. Research on expressed emotion (Leff, 2001; Leff and Vaughn, 1981), for example, showed the impact of family environment on relapse rates of family members with schizophrenia. Family intervention models were needed that could better address the family's ability to construct an environment that would be supportive of the person with schizophrenia and be aware of the stress and isolation many families experience when trying to cope with this illness.

In the late 1970s and early 1980s, Michael Goldstein, Ian Falloon, and Carol Anderson and her colleagues were hard at work developing such models of family intervention. Some of the models, Falloon's in particular, were greatly influenced by the behavioral family therapy models previously discussed. Much of this work came together in 1986 with the publication of *Schizophrenia and the Family: A Practitioner's Guide to Psychoeducation and Management* (Anderson, Reiss, and Hogarty). This book became the primary source for the continued development and refinement of the psychoeducational model. The book outlines the basic concepts that shape the model and presents a concrete process for conducting psychoeducational interventions.

Application to Schizophrenia

The main concept that shapes the psychoeducational model is the belief that families are not pathological, and that they are not the cause of schizophrenia. Families coping with schizophrenia, however, are often burned out, overwhelmed, and depleted of resources (financial, emotional, psychological, social, etc.). Many families have struggled, often alone, to try to do the best they can in the face of a very troubling illness. They have had to struggle with an often confusing patchwork of mental health services, a confusing array of private and public funding for services, and the uncertainty of the illness itself. The psychoeducational model tries to reach out to families and help alleviate some of these experiences.

The psychoeducational model takes a very collaborative approach with families. Through structured meetings and other interventions, it provides support, empowerment, and accurate information about schizophrenia. By focusing on the strengths each family possesses and building on those, the model's primary goal is to create a family environment that prevents or reduces the frequency and severity of relapse episodes. Support is achieved through meeting with other families who are coping with similar issues. Focusing on and supporting the strengths in the family and giving families accurate information about the illness and the mental health system helps them achieve empowerment. Such knowledge helps families better understand the illness and negotiate the system in a more proactive manner. Similar to self-help programs, the psychoeducational model firmly believes that knowledge is power. A well-informed family can better deal with stigma, the illness, and the various mental health professionals.

ESSENTIAL SKILLS AND TECHNIQUES

Dissemination of Information

The primary skill used in psychoeducational intervention is the dissemination of information. Whether in the form of a more didactic presentation or in a question and answer format, the leaders try to provide family members with accurate, up-to-date information about the various aspects of schizophrenia and its impact on the family. Very often the information concerns itself with better understanding the illness (e.g., etiology, diagnosis, course, and treatment), issues surrounding the use of psychotropic medication (e.g., compliance, side effects), and specific coping strategies for the family (e.g., problem-solving skills, assertiveness, limit-setting).

Readjusting Expectations

Through the provision of knowledge and group discussion, psychoeducational intervention tries to readjust the expectations the family may have toward the person with schizophrenia. For example, questions may arise about how much responsibility the person with schizophrenia should have for completing household chores, tending to personal hygiene, taking medication, or even working. One family may feel that more structure and tasks can help fill the person's day and provide a sense of purpose, but another family feels the person with schizophrenia should have no expectations placed on him or her for fear of creating too much stress and anxiety. Both extremes may be incorrect depending on where the person with schizophrenia is in his or her illness. Such expectations need to be adjusted based on a better understanding of the illness in general and the specific needs of each family in particular.

Collaboration

Psychoeducational intervention also seeks to build a collaborative relationship between family members to help decrease feelings of burnout and isolation. In many families living with schizophrenia, the responsibility of caring for the person with schizophrenia often falls on one person's shoulders. Often this is one parent or an older sibling. By involving the entire family in the process, the family can learn ways to share any burdens, share resources to increase options for the family, and reach out to each other in supportive ways. Psychoeducational intervention sometimes follows the traditional structural family therapy model and focuses on the hierarchy within the family and the various subsystems at work. Special attention may be made of the unique needs of parents and of siblings. Each subsystem may experience different types of stress and stigma. For example, a younger sibling may worry about what his or her friends will say if they find out the family has a member with schizophrenia. Feelings of shame, isolation, fear, and anger may be difficult for the younger sibling to acknowledge or manage.

Building Social Supports

Similar to the multiple family group intervention mentioned in Chapter 12, psychoeducational intervention can also build social supports. This often happens in at least two ways. First, the model encourages families to reach out to others, such as extended family members, or involve themselves with self-help or family advocacy programs (see Chapter 14), as a way of building a broader range of social support. Second, as the families attend the various meetings as part of the psychoeducational intervention, they naturally begin to talk with each other, see others who are struggling with similar issues, and often begin to form bonds with some of the other families present. These connections often continue outside of the meetings and long after the intervention has concluded.

Flexibility

Finally, because each family has its own idiosyncratic needs, the psychoeducational intervention tries to address such needs in a flexible manner. Many times issues may arise that have little to do with schizophrenia but speak more to how the family is coping with other issues. For example, the medical illness of a parent, the loss of a job, or the death of a relative can all have an impact on the family's stress level, resources, and ability to cope. Although the psychoeducational intervention does not set out to identify such issues ahead of time, they do arise in the normal course of the intervention. Those clinicians who lead psychoeducational programs must be attuned for such possibilities and have the family-intervention skills necessary to help the family address and resolve these types of issues.

THE PROCESS OF FAMILY THERAPY

The model by Anderson, Reiss, and Hogarty (1986) outlines a specific four-stage process to their psychoeducational model. Other models may provide some variation on this theme but still provide a very concrete process and curriculum. It is this clear structure that makes the psychoeducational model user friendly and more easily provided to families in a variety of settings. The model follows the following five stages: connecting with the families, providing the survival skills workshop, reentry (continued family work for about one year), social and vocational rehabilitation, and the final stage that focuses on success of meeting goals and the establishment of stable functioning.

Connecting with the Families

Connecting with the families provides the base for all of the work to come. The authors set out five goals for the connecting phase, goals that should be found in all work with families living with schizophrenia:

1. Develop a collaborative working alliance
2. Assess the family to better understand what problems might exist that contribute to stress within the family
3. Find out about family resources and how the family has tried to cope with the illness both past and present
4. Assess for and build on family strengths
5. Establish a contract with the family that sets out the rules and expectations of treatment and the specific goals the family wants to accomplish

Providing the Survival Skills Workshop

The workshop becomes an important focal point of the psychoeducational model. The main goal is to provide the family with extensive information about the illness of schizophrenia and family-related issues. The authors even provide a sample outline of a workshop for other clinicians to follow. The workshop covers the history and experience of schizophrenia, the treatment of the illness, family reactions to schizophrenia, what families can do to help, and question and answer time for specific family concerns. Workshops are often conducted by mental health professionals and may include presentations by family members who have gone through the program in the past.

Reentry

The reentry stage helps the family begin to put into practice what was learned in the workshop. Usually following the discharge from the hospital of the relative with schizophrenia, the family as a whole begins to meet with the clinician. The continued meetings help the family and person with schizophrenia integrate back into the environment outside of the hospital and begin the process of moving the person with schizophrenia toward social and vocational goals.

Social and Vocational Rehabilitation

The social and vocational rehabilitation stage starts when the person with schizophrenia has been able to maintain himself or herself outside of the hospital and has reintegrated back into the family by fulfilling some responsibilities within the family. Although the social and vocational goals will vary due to the severity of the illness, some expectations for reintegration back into the community through social networks and work should be developed. This stage breaks the process of social and vocational rehabilitation down into very manageable goals. For example, with social rehabilitation, the model suggests starting with outings with the family, followed by more independent outings, followed by outings with others (e.g., peers). Along the way, the family should begin to develop some regular family activities that help the person with schizophrenia feel a part of the family.

Meeting Goals and Establishing Stable Functioning

The final stage of the model depends on how well the family and the person with schizophrenia have accomplished the goals set out in the original contract. Obviously each family will move at a different pace depending on the severity of the illness, family resources, and family strengths. As goals are accomplished other goals may develop, leading to a renegotiation of the treatment contract. The concerns discussed within the family sessions may change, focusing less on issues related to living with schizophrenia and more on sibling issues, parental issues, or other larger-systems issues.

Anderson, Reiss, and Hogarty (1986) point out that termination is a complicated issue. As there is no cure for schizophrenia, the family and the person with the illness will continue to struggle with issues and stresses. Many families may choose to terminate only to return to treatment when a particular issue arises which tests the resolve of the family and the person with schizophrenia. For other families, some kind of ongoing, intermittent meetings are preferable to help them negotiate the long-term nature of the illness. The clinician and the family need to discuss the pros and cons of termination and what fits the specific needs of the family.

Conclusion

What does the future hold for the psychoeducational intervention? As with the multiple family group intervention, the future is very bright. Although I have raised some criticisms about the psychoeducational model (Marley, 1992), my concern was not about the basic concept and theory but about some of the technical aspects. Overall, the research has been overwhelming in supporting the psychoeducational model as an important method of intervention that should be more widely utilized. Also, with the cross-fertilization occurring between multiple family group therapy, psychoeducational interventions, and cognitive-behavioral models, it is expected that each of these models will benefit from the interaction and develop new mechanisms to help families. Any agency interested in providing interventions for families living with schizophrenia would be expected to include the psychoeducational process as a fundamental part of its offerings. The model is very clear, robust, and has much to offer families.

Chapter 14

Self-Help and Advocacy: NAMI and Recovery, Inc.

BRIEF OVERVIEW AND APPLICATION TO SCHIZOPHRENIA

It is beyond the scope or purpose of this book to examine in detail the history of the self-help movement in mental health. Other resources cover the topic in more detail (e.g., Norcross et al., 2000). However, self-help programs and family advocacy organizations have played a key role in the long-term care of individuals with schizophrenia and their family members. In particular, throughout the twentieth century, a number of groups and organizations, some well organized and others with more informal structures, have been filling in the gaps of professional mental health services. In many cases, the groups and organizations have played a leadership role in the development of new knowledge about schizophrenia, the wide dissemination of this knowledge to public and professionals alike, encouraged better funding for research and services, and helped develop legislation that has directly affected those with schizophrenia and their family members. The grassroots nature of these programs often makes them very attractive to family members who may have had difficult relationships with mental health professionals over the years.

Because many of these programs are new, informal, or tied to a very specific geographic area, the availability of literature about them may be limited unless you have access to a self-help organization clearinghouse. Such clearinghouses are becoming more available through the World Wide Web. Two resources are The National Self-Help Clearinghouse at <www.selfhelpweb.org> and the National Mental Health Consumer's Self-Help Clearinghouse at <www.mhselfhelp.org>.

However, two programs with a more substantial history and a more widely disseminated literature provide good examples of how such programs can operate. Both organizations operate very user-friendly Web sites and produce very good newsletters where much of the following information was gathered.

The National Alliance for the Mentally Ill (NAMI)

The National Alliance for the Mentally Ill (NAMI) is probably the largest and most well-organized consumer-oriented family advocacy program in the country. Founded in 1979, it now has over 200,000 members. The organization has affiliates throughout the United States, Canada, and Puerto Rico. NAMI has worked with people in Australia and Japan to form related organizations. NAMI defines itself as "a nonprofit, grassroots, self-help, support and advocacy organization of consumers, families, and friends of people with severe mental illnesses, such as schizophrenia, major depression, bipolar disorder, obsessive-compulsive disorder, and anxiety disorders." NAMI defines severe mental illnesses as physical brain disorders, and has played a leadership role in trying to dispel some of the myths and unfounded theories about the causes of these illnesses. Much of the up-to-date information about NAMI in this book came from the organization's Web site.

Recovery, Inc. (RI)

Recovery, Inc. (RI), was founded in 1937 and is based on the theory and writings of Abraham A. Low (1891-1954). Dr. Low was a neuropsychiatrist in Chicago in the 1930s when he developed a specific form of self-help psychotherapy. His work began to focus on the aftercare of former mental patients and what their relatives needed to know to be helpful to the recovery process. In the early 1940s, Low began to systematize his ideas about recovery and the role of self-help groups in the process. By the mid-to-late 1940s, the self-help component of Low's work, RI, was publishing manuals dedicated to his work and the process of recovery from mental illness.

Low's main theory focused on two components, *temper* and *symptoms*. Temper was divided into anger and fear. If a person perceived himself or herself to be wrong, this was called fearful temper. If the person perceived someone else to be wrong it was called angry temper. Low hypothesized that the only difference between normal symptoms and pathological symptoms were their intensity, duration, and the element of danger associated with the symptoms. Low hypothesized a connection between temper, tension, and symptoms. Temper causes tension and tension causes symptoms. A change in temper could reduce the experience of tension and then reduce the pathological symptoms.

Recovery, Inc. has developed as the primary mechanism through which Low's theories are translated into a self-help program. RI provides consumers the components of a recovery program. The program involves learning techniques that help change the way the individual interacts with others, manages problematic thoughts, feelings, and behaviors, and reduces the experience of tension and the symptoms caused by it. The individual learns the program by attending groups, reading the literature, and practicing the techniques outside of the group. Information about Recovery, Inc., can be obtained at its Web site <www. recovery-inc.com>.

ESSENTIAL SKILLS AND TECHNIQUES

NAMI

The issue of skills and techniques is obviously different when discussing self-help and advocacy programs compared to family therapy models. Yet both organizations have operating principles and a defined purpose to their work. For NAMI, their main principle seems to be that knowledge and numbers mean empowerment. The more that families and consumers know about mental illness and mental health services, and the more families and consumers who are involved at the local, state, and national level in advocating for people with severe mental illness, then the more power and control these families and consumers will have over their care. To reach this end they are organized around four key components: support, education, advocacy, and research.

Support is achieved through group meetings NAMI sponsors around the country that allow family members to meet and discuss issues and concerns with each other and with mental health professionals. NAMI also provides a telephone number that people can call to get information about a variety of mental illnesses, NAMI programs, and NAMI policy statements (1-800-950-6264). The phone number can also direct callers to local NAMI affiliates for more direct contact.

Education is achieved through a number of outlets within the organization. NAMI provides a number of publications about severe mental illness and family issues. Also, NAMI reviews and recommends a number of professional and consumer-oriented books about mental illness. NAMI has developed what it refers to as a "family-to-family education program." The program consists of a twelve-week course, similar to a psychoeducational program, but is taught by trained family members as opposed to mental health professionals. The merging of psychoeducation with self-help provides families with essential information in an environment that is less stressful and that provides a ready-made support group.

NAMI's policy goals are achieved through the organization's *advocacy* for passage of a number of pieces of legislation that focus on mental health issues. Such legislation includes research priorities, access to services, and parity in insurance coverage for treatment of mental illness. NAMI has been very successful in making the needs of its members heard in the development and passage of state and national laws that directly affect people with mental illness and their family members.

The two main *research* goals of NAMI are to disseminate information about advances in research on mental illness and to provide information about research studies and how individuals with mental illness and their family members can participate. NAMI provides information about the research studies, and the organization's research board screens the studies before listing them for their members. NAMI has also developed their own policy issues related to research on people with severe mental illness.

Taken as a whole, these four components help NAMI achieve its stated goals and mission. The organization has focused itself on the education of and advocacy for people with severe mental illness and their family members. The growth in its membership since its inception indicates that consumers and family members are receptive to the organization and what it has to offer.

RI

RI shares some similarities with NAMI in its goals and objectives. RI is primarily focused on helping the person with a mental illness learn a set of coping skills. The meetings run by RI allow individuals to discuss specific events that triggered a problematic response, how the self-help techniques help diffuse the situation, and how the situation might have turned out if the person did not know the self-help techniques. Low was very clear in his work, and RI has followed suit that the self-help method is an adjunct to professional care. It is believed that a consumer who learns the self-help skills will be better able to manage the illness and, therefore, be a better collaborator with the mental health professional in treatment planning and treatment compliance. Unlike NAMI, the target population for RI is much broader. Although it includes people who have been diagnosed with schizophrenia, other psychotic disorders, and bipolar disorder, it also includes people diagnosed with personality disorders, dysthymia, anxiety, and obsessive-compulsive disorders. Some people who have no formal diagnosis but simply want to learn new coping skills have attended RI groups.

The RI groups meet an additional goal by providing a social support network for the individual. Trained volunteers run all RI meetings. Many of the volunteers have had some form of mental health problem and utilize the self-help techniques of RI. During the meeting, the participants usually listen to a taped lecture by Dr. Low or read passages from his work. Participants have the chance to discuss how they are applying the techniques to their daily lives. More informal discussions can take place among members in an effort to provide each other with additional support.

In an effort to reach out to family members and friends who care for someone with a mental illness, RI developed the Relatives Project. Simply put, the Relatives Project attempts to export Low's theory and techniques to these groups in an effort to create a healthier environment at home for the person with the mental illness. Family members and friends have the opportunity to learn how to manage their own tensions through the self-help methods of RI. The Relatives Project is still somewhat new to RI and is available in only a few selected areas of the country. The project is being evaluated with the hope of expanding its availability in the future.

Contacting NAMI and RI

National Alliance for the Mentally Ill
Colonial Place Three
2107 Wilson Blvd., Suite 300
Arlington, VA 22201-3042
Phone: 703-524-7600
Fax: 703-524-9094
Web site: <www.nami.org>
NAMI HelpLine: 1-800-950-6264

Recovery, Inc.
802 North Dearborn St.
Chicago, IL 60610
Phone: 312-337-5661
Fax: 312-337-5667
Web site: <www.recovery-inc.com>

Chapter 15

What the Research Tells Us

ISSUES IN CONDUCTING RESEARCH ON FAMILY INTERVENTION MODELS

Sprenkle and Moon (1996) sum up the state of research in family therapy by pointing out that

> Although family therapy is now more than 50 years old, it is safe to say that the rapid growth of the field has depended more on its intuitive appeal than on solid research evidence for its efficacy. It is still possible for a highly charismatic individual to develop a model of family therapy, get book contracts to promulgate it, and become successful on the workshop circuit without offering a scintilla of evidence beyond testimonials for the efficacy of the model. Although there are some indications that the tide may be turning, the field remains vulnerable because of its lack of attention to developing a solid foundation of research on the process and outcomes of family therapy. (p. 3)

Is this the same case for family therapy as it applies to schizophrenia? The answer is yes and no. Yes in the sense that many models discussed throughout this book lack solid research evidence to support their claims to be an effective model of intervention. No in the sense that at least for the past twenty years, several models have received extensive research scrutiny and support. The findings from this research are discussed later in the text. However, it is important to first recognize some of the fundamental problems associated with conducting research on family therapy. The main problems center on two questions: (1) What is being researched? and (2) How is it being researched?

What Is Being Researched?

The first question may sound odd since we are talking about family therapy in general and family therapy applied to schizophrenia in particular. Yet the question is fundamental and problematic. Family therapy as practiced and researched exists on at least five levels of abstraction. The basic schema looks similar to this:

Paradigm → Theory → Model → Technique → Action

A *paradigm* is the overarching belief system or epistemology out of which comes the understanding of the concept of family, and how the clinician or researcher comes to know about the concept. It is at the highest level of abstraction. *Theories* emerge out of a paradigm. The theories may be about family functioning, how families come to look and act the way they do, and the various assumptions made about individual and family dynamics. The *model,* then, becomes the articulation of the underlying theory where the assumptions are made explicit. The model presents a unified conceptualization of etiology and recommends action a family therapist can take to work with a specific family. Most models address the issue of action by presenting a number of *techniques* a family therapist can follow to bring about change or activity in the family therapy session. *Action,* then, becomes that actual behavior of the therapist and the family during their experience together. In the best of all possible worlds, there is a logical flow or connection from the highest level of abstraction (paradigm) to the most basic unit of behavior (action).

The problem with conducting research on the models of family therapy presented in this book is that there is often uneven development in these five levels. One model may be very strong at articulating its theoretical basis, but is weak when it comes to presenting specific techniques for action. Another model may have numerous techniques to offer, but does so in the absence of any underlying theoretical context. Some models may be more balanced in their development.

When conducting research to evaluate the effectiveness of a model, the researcher must be clear about which level of abstraction is actually the unit of analysis. Is it the model, or some specific techniques, or some behavior that emerges in the family therapy session itself? This issue is particularly problematic when trying to compare two models of family therapy. It is, in general, easier to conduct research on the lower-level abstractions (techniques and actions). It is much harder to conduct research on the higher-level abstractions.

In a related issue, since many models of family therapy emerge out of a common paradigm and related theories, it becomes conceptually confusing to conduct research that compares models of family therapy. With theory overlap comes model overlap and overlap in techniques. Therefore, it is difficult to isolate a model for research and indicate that it is fundamentally different from the other model for comparison. Such forced differentiation often leads to unrealistic family therapy experiences for the clients that do not reflect what actually happens in family therapy.

How Is It Being Researched?

The second question has been addressed in the literature more recently. Sprenkle and Moon (1996) indicate the field has gone through two major shifts in its history. First, the field adopted a more quantifiable and experimental approach to research. Such an approach gave this new field some research respectability, and forced practitioners to take a hard look at some of their concepts and beliefs which required better articulation to hold up to research procedures. The second major shift was "from a strict adherence to quantitative methods to incorporation and gradual acceptance of alternative methodologies, especially qualitative ones" (p. 4). Such a shift followed the general influence of postmodern philosophical beliefs and their influence on a number of disciplines, professions, and research. Often referred to as constructivism, the theory presented a challenge to the notion of an "objective truth" that can be quantified, isolated, and studied. Unfortunately, the field of family therapy research soon joined other disciplines and professions in the formation of two camps, the quantitative researchers and the qualitative (or constructionist) researchers. Such a forced dichotomy in the research field does nothing but obscure the main issue at hand: How do we know if a specific approach to working with families is better than doing nothing and is better than some other approach to working with families? Although "objectivist" and "constructivist" approaches emerge out of different paradigms, both can be useful depending on the specific research question being asked. The "pluralism" that Sprenkle and Moon (1996) advocate, respecting and utilizing both objective and constructive approaches, gives family therapy researchers the best opportunity to ask the important questions and then choose the appropriate methodology to find the answers.

OVERVIEW OF RESEARCH FINDINGS

It would be safe to say that the published research on family intervention in the treatment of schizophrenia is a relatively recent phenomenon. A quick Internet search (December, 2002) using PubMed revealed the following information. Using the search term "family therapy" turned up 5,311 citations. Altering the search term to "family therapy AND research" yielded 641 citations. Finally, altering the search term to "family therapy AND research AND schizophrenia" turned up 101 citations. This discussion utilizes information from some of these 101 citations, a modest percentage of the overall literature on family therapy in general and family therapy research in particular. The oldest citation was for an article published in the early 1960s. The most recent was from the year 2002. The vast majority of the published research was from the 1980s onward. Not surprisingly, most of the research focused on behavioral family therapy, multiple family therapy, and various psychoeducational approaches.

For the most part, no empirical support exists for the following family therapies as they apply to schizophrenia: psychoanalytic, Bowenian, experiential, structural, strategic, systemic, narrative, and solution-focused. Does that mean these models have no utility in the treatment of schizophrenia?

The answer would have to be no, for several reasons. First, the lack of empirical support may have more to do with the interests of clinicians and researchers than with any fundamental flaw in the theory or model. As mentioned before, many second- and third-generation family therapists who were trained within one or more of these models have moved away from playing an active role in the treatment of schizophrenia.

Second, some of these models have been useful in treating other conditions, indicating some inherent strength of the model. In particular, structural family therapy showed good success in treating anorexia nervosa (Minuchin, Rosman, and Baker, 1978), strategic family therapy has made inroads in treating addiction (Stanton and Todd,

1982), and experiential family therapy has been useful in working with some couples issues (Greenberg and Johnson, 1988). Such research has led to the operationalization of some of the "fuzzy" concepts found in many of these models. The research also indicates empirical evaluation is possible if the clinician is committed to pursuing such a line of inquiry. Narrative and solution-focused are relatively new models; hopefully more rigorous evaluation will occur in the future.

A third, more complicated issue is the nature of anecdotal research in the evaluation of a model. Many of the previous models have a wealth of support in the form of case studies, observational reports, and family therapist reports. Is this sufficient for evaluation and support? In particular, the family therapists operating within the narrative theory come from a paradigm that challenges the primacy of empirical evaluation. How do they gain support for their model and work with people with schizophrenia? The pluralism previously discussed in how family therapy can be evaluated is critical to this question. A reliance on empirical research as the only gauge for effectiveness may limit the types of family therapy models implemented and tested in treating schizophrenia.

The empirical research is much more prevalent when evaluating the following models of family intervention with schizophrenia: behavioral, psychoeducational, and multiple family therapy. In fact, a tremendous amount of cross-fertilization occurred among these three models. For example, Ian Falloon, one of the major writers on behavioral family therapy, has played an important role in the development of psychoeducational models. William McFarlane, who played an important role in the development of MFGT, has now merged the traditional structure of MFGT with psychoeducational components.

Several research studies on behavioral family therapy and schizophrenia were discussed by Falloon and Liberman (1983). In particular, their studies on personal effectiveness training and home-based family therapy showed both methods had a significant impact on developing better communication skills and decreasing relapse. More recently, Muesur and Glynn (1999) have shown behavioral family therapy to be an effective intervention when working with schizophrenia and other severe mental illnesses.

Psychoeducational models of family intervention have also received strong empirical support. Most recently, studies by Bustillo et al. (2001) and Dixon, Adams, and Lucksted (2000) found the data supporting psychoeducational interventions to be overwhelming.

Research on Multiple Family Group Therapy (MFGT) began in the 1960s and continues to this day. Two previous comprehensive literature reviews (Strenlick, 1978; O'Shea and Phelps, 1985) and McFarlane's (2002) own work continue to demonstrate the model's effectiveness. McFarlane (2002) devotes an entire chapter to the empirical support for multifamily group interventions. Some of the findings show such interventions decrease relapse rates and increase vocational rehabilitation rates.

Research on the effectiveness of self-help and family advocacy programs is somewhat problematic. First, many of the services are run by nonprofessionals who may not see research as useful or relevant to what they are trying to accomplish. Second, the population that makes use of such services is often more difficult to study as their involvement may be sporadic. Third, since most self-help and family advocacy programs have many components, it is difficult to operationalize these programs and components as discrete variables for study. Finally, many people who make use of such services may not want it known they are receiving such services. Many families still report concerns about stigma and fear if their employers, neighbors, or relatives find out about the mental illness. Although this seems contrary to what self-help and family advocacy programs are trying to accomplish, stigma and fear are still very real concerns for many families.

There is some empirical support for components of NAMI, in particular their family-to-family program (Dixon et al., 2001). Also, there is some research on self-help in general that is applicable to NAMI and Recovery, Inc. Mowbray and Tan (1993) found in a study of mental health consumers in Michigan that the vast majority were very satisfied with the self-help programs they utilized. This is in keeping with other studies conducted in other geographic areas that have reached the same conclusion. Yanos, Primavera, and Knight (2001) found that participants in consumer-run programs had better social functioning than those in traditional mental health services. To help facilitate research on self-help programs in the future, Segal, Redman, and Silverman (2000) developed an assessment tool specifically designed to measure satisfaction with self-help services. Such a tool may allow for more consistency in the research, thus leading to better cross comparisons between different types of self-help groups.

This kind of research is needed. Toro (1990) feels that self-help programs do not get evaluated fairly (when they get evaluated at all) because they are not run by professionals. Segal, Silverman, and Temkin (1993) note that even with the tremendous growth of self-help programs, there are still a number of questions about their process and accomplishments that require further study.

PRACTICE IMPLICATIONS

Taken as a whole, the research literature on family interventions with schizophrenia is weak (in some areas) but getting better. With time there will be, hopefully, more studies looking at the effectiveness and efficacy of various models that approach the evaluation process from a multitude of perspectives. Such evaluations need to include the input of the families and the individuals with schizophrenia and should demonstrate the model's utility under normal clinical conditions. It would not be surprising, however, to see only a few models receive such ongoing critical evaluation and other models languish for lack of research. One force that may drive such a trend is the push to fund services that only utilize "best practice models." This trend may force clinicians who utilize third-party payers to be reimbursed only if they offer certain prescribed family interventions.

For practitioners who are interested in family intervention models, the research strongly suggests looking first at the psychoeducational, multiple family group, and cognitive-behavioral models. In particular, the first two mentioned, and the integrated model that includes components of both, are perhaps the easiest to begin with for clinicians new to this area. However, as is pointed out throughout this book, each model has something to offer families who are living with schizophrenia. In the end, the practitioner will have to decide for himself or herself which model best fits his or her own clinical style and meets the needs of the families who come for service.

Chapter 16

Professional Issues

DEVELOPING A "FAMILY FOCUS" FROM SCRATCH

Depending on your familiarity with family therapy, or with the illness of schizophrenia, you may be wondering just how to get started in doing this kind of work. Although the various models presented throughout this book can provide a framework for understanding family intervention in schizophrenia, you may want a more specific game plan that will be easier to implement. Such a game plan would allow you the opportunity to develop a "family focus" in your agency or institution, and pursue staff development and training to hone their family intervention skills. In the process of lecturing to numerous groups of mental health professionals and groups of families who are struggling to cope with schizophrenia, I have devised a five-step program for developing such a focus. The following is an outline of each step, with suggestions for finding published material to help you along the way.

Step One

Develop, advertise, and provide a psychoeducational program to families in your area who are coping with a relative with mental illness. The literature is replete with psychoeducational curricula such that you can adopt one of the programs to fit your agency or institution's specific needs. In particular, the foundational work of Anderson, Reiss, and Hogarty (1986) can provide you with a standard approach. Such programs are well documented in the research literature (Dixon and Lehman, 1995) as being very effective. Most of the psychoeducational curricula focus on the following topics: understanding the signs and symptoms of specific types of severe mental illness; the use and effectiveness of various treatments; an overview of psychiatric medications and their side effects; issues specific to family coping such as dealing with stress, stigma, problem solving, etc.; and resources such as self-help and consumer advocacy groups that can provide ongoing support for these families. Most of these programs allow plenty of time for questions from and discussion with the families about specific concerns. One of the advantages of this type of program is that it allows the families to meet and interact with the staff in a more informal and less-stressful environment.

Step Two

Encourage all of the families who attend, and those who cannot, to join the local or state affiliate of the NAMI or one of the other major family advocacy groups. Families should be actively encouraged to explore membership in one of the major family support and advocacy organizations. In addition to providing additional information about mental illness and coping skills, such organizations help families feel less isolated. Many have specific programs designed to connect families to each other for the purposes of support and education. By getting on the mailing lists of these organizations, or via the Internet and e-mail, families can continue to receive important information on medications, treatment strategies, important books, and changes in state and federal laws that may have an impact on the kind of care available to their relative with a mental illness.

Step Three

Recruit from those families who attend the psychoeducational program a sufficient number of families to begin one or more multiple family groups. Provided your agency or institution has the resources, beginning a multiple family group is a good way to focus on more specific family needs and dynamics. As previously discussed, there is very good documentation in the practice and research literature to support the use of such a program. Although these groups require more professional skills and preparation, most clinicians who have an active interest in providing this service can digest the published material and plan the development of a group. Advantages of a multiple family group include connecting families to one another in a more meaningful way, providing families with more specific information and feedback about their unique struggles, and allowing families to help one another by sharing their experiences.

Step Four

Refer families who want more individualized attention to your primary family clinicians. As a final service, identify who your primary family clinicians are and refer specific families to these individuals. These may be professionals with advanced training in family therapy or who are in the process of learning the fundamentals of family therapy. The material covered through the majority of this book can provide such clinicians with guidance toward specific models and literature to help inform their development in this service. Some clinicians may want to seek out programs designed to train people in family therapy. Such programs exist across the country. The American Association of Marriage and Family Therapy (AAMFT) can be one resource for identifying these programs in your area.

Step Five

Obtain professional consultation in developing any or all of the previous steps. There are many professionals from various professional disciplines who specialize in some or all of these types of services. Often, they are available for discussion and consultation in guiding you in the development of these services. The authors of many of the references cited in this book are active researchers and clinicians who continue to publish in this area and present at various national and regional conferences. If all goes well, you may be able to have an agency or institution that has a full array of family-focused services designed to meet the various needs of families coping with severe mental illness.

TRAINING AND PROFESSIONAL SKILL BUILDING

What are the specific training and skill-building needs of clinicians who decide to work with people with schizophrenia from a family orientation? Cole and Cole (1987) provide a basic overview of some of the key issues involved in the development of a well-qualified clinician. First, the clinician will have to understand the nature of schizophrenia. This includes theories about its cause, impact on the individual and family, and the treatment (including psychopharmacologic interventions) currently available. Second, the clinician will have to understand the nature of the family that is trying to cope with schizophrenia. This includes the family's developmental cycle, coping strategies, the role of stigma and stress on the family, and the role of self-help and family advocacy in supporting the family. Third, the clinician will have to understand the nature of the mental health care system within which the individual and family exist. This includes knowledge of insurance and other economic supports for accessing care, the types of structures within which the care can be offered (e.g., state hospitals, community mental health centers, and rehabilitation centers), and how the various structures and economic issues can impact on the family and individual trying to cope with schizophrenia.

Once this basic knowledge is gained, the clinician then needs to learn how to work with these families. This work involves achieving two main goals: developing an attitude that invites and promotes family participation in the treatment of schizophrenia and developing the skills necessary to work with the family from a particular approach. This book can be a starting point for achieving the second goal. The first goal is a bit more complicated. If the clinician has some family intervention skills, just not with families living with schizophrenia, the issue may be more about becoming comfortable working with a person with schizophrenia. Spending time at an inpatient psychiatric unit or partial hospital program may help sensitize the clinician to some of the issues in working with these individuals. If the clinician has never worked with families before, he or she should seek out qualified clinical supervision and consultation before taking on many family cases.

SUPERVISION AND CONSULTATION

The effective provision of family services in the treatment of schizophrenia relies heavily on the ability of the clinician to have access to quality clinical supervision and consultation. Because of the nature of the illness, the tremendous stress and anxiety many of these families experience, and the often slow rate of progress due to the severity of the illness, clinicians and agencies need to be aware of the potential for burnout. Effective supervision and case consultation can be provided by a clinician who has experience working with families living with schizophrenia. The supervision and consultation should include the following, at a minimum:

1. Discussions about the nature of the illness of schizophrenia to ensure the clinician is up-to-date with changes in the field
2. Discussions about family intervention models, their strengths and weaknesses, to ensure the clinician is providing the best possible intervention that meets the specific needs of the family
3. Discussion of specific cases to see how well the clinician is carrying out the treatment plan, engaging the family, and, hopefully, building on family strengths
4. Self-reflection on the part of the clinician to ensure he or she is not bringing into the sessions any counterproductive beliefs about schizophrenia, stigma, family blame, or other troubling issues
5. Helping the clinician develop an assessment strategy to better monitor each family's progress and the overall effectiveness of the clinician's interventions

In the mental health field, as in other fields, good quality supervision is an absolute necessity. Unfortunately, it is not always readily available in some agencies and institutions. Also, because of the decreased interest of many family therapists in working with families living with schizophrenia, it may be harder to find quality supervisors who are knowledgeable about this specific area. For those clinicians who have a strong interest in this area of practice, it may be necessary to find someone outside the agency or institution who can provide supervision or case consultation on a fee-for-service basis. The clinician should determine whether the agency or institution has any mechanism available to help offset the cost of such outside professional development.

ETHICAL ISSUES AND GUIDELINES

Each professional who finds himself or herself providing family services in the treatment of schizophrenia is expected to follow the code of ethics of his or her profession. Each specific code may vary in some of its expectations, and each code needs to be integrated into the general ethical environment of the agency or institution. In particular, it is important for the clinician to determine how open the agency or institution is in discussing and processing ethical dilemmas faced by the clinician in the provision of services to families coping with schizophrenia.

Two specific areas covered by most codes of ethics need to be addressed. Those aspects of the code that address practice often require or imply that the clinician is providing an effective intervention that is within his or her scope of competency. This requires that the clinician have knowledge about the intervention, its research support, and that the skills required to provide the intervention are skills possessed by the clinician. To fulfill such an ethical expectation requires the clinician to be knowledgeable about the literature on family interventions with schizophrenia and be active in his or her own professional development. There are a number of journals that frequently publish work in this area. Three I have relied on heavily in the past include *Schizophrenia Bulletin, Psychiatric Services,* and *Psychiatric Rehabilitation Journal*. Other journals such as the *American Journal of Orthopsychiatry* and some of the family therapy journals publish work in this area periodically.

Those aspects of the code that address research often require the clinician to both evaluate his or her own practice effectiveness and to take special care when conducting research on a more broad basis. In particular, the research expectation called "informed consent" can be a troubling issue when working with families coping with schizophrenia. Informed consent implies that the person you are doing research on understands in general the nature of the research, what is expected of him or her, any risks in undertaking to participate in the research, and that he or she can withdraw without penalty from the research. For people with the diagnosis of schizophrenia, the researcher must be careful to weigh the needs of the research against the care and rehabilitation of the person with the illness. Also, the illness of schizophrenia may impair the individual to such an extent that he or she cannot give informed consent. Those clinicians who want a better understanding of some of these research-related issues are encouraged to consult some of the texts available that focus on research with vulnerable populations (e.g., Dworkin, 1992).

Chapter 17

Future Developments

"DOING TO, DOING FOR, AND DOING WITH" THE FAMILIES

Families coping with schizophrenia and the mental health professionals they seek out for services have been intertwined in a unique dance. In the past, mental health professionals have led the dance and called the tune. The family members, including the individual with schizophrenia, have been relegated to a marginalized position. They have tolerated misinformation, poor services and treatment, and often hostile attitudes from those who are supposed to help them. Their passive role as recipient of whatever the professional's thought was best added to their isolation and powerlessness in the face of a devastating illness.

In the 1960s and early 1970s, a slightly more collaborative approach emerged to working with families coping with schizophrenia. This was not a true partnership. Most professionals still felt they were in charge and possessed unique training and knowledge that families did not possess. Professionals, as the experts, could give their help to those families in need.

The end of the 1970s and beginning of the 1980s saw the development of a more collaborative relationship between families and family therapists who were interested in working with severe mental illness. The formation and growth of NAMI, new developments such as the strengths perspective in the helping professions, and the general growth of a "consumer" attitude toward helping professionals, empowered more families to take a collaborative stance. Families were seen as the experts of their own life situation, and models of family therapy emerged that respected that notion and utilized it in its process of helping.

What is the next step in this developing dance between family and mental health professionals? Is the collaborative model the best it can get? One development still gaining momentum is the psychiatric rehabilitation perspective. Championed by such organizations as the International Association of Psychosocial Rehabilitation Services (www.iapsrs.org), including the development of a new certification program for people who want to be Certified Psychiatric Rehabilitation Professionals (CPRP), it focuses on consumer empowerment, collaborative work with families, and a positive/strengths-based attitude toward working with people with severe mental illnesses. It would seem logical to assume that the continued growth of the consumer empowerment movement and the recovery movement coupled with ongoing research on the effectiveness of family interventions will merge into a new service delivery. Perhaps this will lead to consumers and their families taking a more active role in the development and provision of family-oriented services.

PROGRESS IN UNDERSTANDING SCHIZOPHRENIA AND IMPACT ON PRACTICE

In 2000 it was announced that the human genome had been decoded. The media discussed this wonderful achievement with extensive newspaper coverage and lengthy segments on the evening news. With little self-restraint, this scientific advance was heralded as a major breakthrough and the first step to understanding and potentially treating most major illness confronting humankind. Once some of the hyperbole dissipated, the media and the public began to truly digest this scientific achievement with some balance and caution. Truly, science has a new tool at its disposal. How useful that tool will be, and how well science can utilize it, remain to be seen. Given that this breakthrough occurred on the heels of the National Institute of Mental Health, "Decade of the Brain," and the numerous developments in understanding the neurophysiology of schizophrenia, you can understand the hope created in the hearts and minds of families everywhere who are affected by schizophrenia.

Yet, in reading much of the literature on this scientific achievement, I could not help but be reminded of an essay by the paleontologist Stephen Jay Gould (2000) and the work of Julian Leff (2001), the social psychiatrist. As Gould so carefully analyzes, the dangers of genetic (or biological) reductionism are numerous and often pervasive. How will mental health professionals incorporate this new information into our understanding and treatment of severe mental illness and not lose sight of the unique environment, culture, and family context within which each person develops? How do we treat a predominantly neurophysiological illness without forgetting the basic humanity of the individual and his or her family? How do we address the role of environment and family without making the past error of blaming one or the other for the presence of the illness? How can we speak meaningfully about a biopsychosocial perspective without our specific bias showing through if we give more weight to one of these three factors involved? How the mental health professionals answer these questions, and the myriad others that will arise, will fundamentally shape how we work with families and how they will work with us.

The "Decade of the Brain" has turned into a much longer phenomenon and has led to important advances in our understanding of the possible etiology of schizophrenia and the development of new medications. Many of these new medications have led mental health professionals to question the usefulness of other types of psychological or social interventions, most notably the role of individual and family interventions. However, as many family members and mental health professionals can attest, these medical breakthroughs have not been without some costs. An example from my own practice, witnessed many times in various settings, can highlight the main concern.

In the early 1990s I was providing consultation and training to a large residential facility that provided long-term care to individuals with severe mental illness. Among the more than 400 individuals who lived in this residence were a handful of young and middle-age people who had not responded well to conventional medication for the treatment of their psychotic symptoms. Some of them, with the financial support of their families, began taking a new antipsychotic medication specifically designed to treat such individuals. The medication was reported to be extremely useful in controlling negative symptoms such as withdrawal and anhedonia. The medication was very expensive due to blood tests that were required to check for a possible serious side effect. Over the course of about a year, a dozen or so individuals began their treatment with this medication. In meetings I held with families periodically there was great hope that this would be the magic medication that would restore their loved one to a much more normal life. And for many of the individuals involved, it did just that. Their thinking cleared, they had more energy, some of their more troubling psychotic symptoms lessened or, in some cases, disappeared altogether. In some cases the change was remarkable and swift. Within a matter of months individuals who had been severely symptomatic for years looked like new people. And then the severe depression hit.

One unintended side effect of the medication was that it led to such a symptom reduction in these individuals that they could now take a clear look around them and take stock of their lives. Many of them did not like what they saw: lost years, lost relationships, lost opportunities, living in a long-term care facility away from their family members, and knowing the stress and strain their symptoms brought to their family. Many of these individuals became severely depressed. Some became suicidal. Their families, so hopeful that the new medication would be the final answer, now needed help understanding the severe depression, its causes, and its consequences. In some cases, those most helped by the new medication wanted to stop taking it because of the depression. Some missed their previous symptoms. Others just did not like the look of their life through nonsymptomatic eyes. In any case, the mental health professionals working with these individuals and their families had to scramble to create new interventions, support groups for example, to manage the depressive symptoms and their fallout.

Was the new medication successful? It certainly alleviated many of the troubling psychotic symptoms. However, medication does not treat the person. It cannot make up for lost time and opportunity. It cannot treat stigma, social isolation, family stress and grief, or myriad other social and environmental consequences of schizophrenia. The biological reductionism taking place in the search for the etiology of schizophrenia, although understandable and necessary, cannot lead to a biological reductionism in how schizophrenia is treated. Once again, this familiar theme of confusing a theory of etiology with a theory of treatment comes to the surface.

MODELS, FAMILIES, AND RESEARCH: CREATIVITY AND INTEGRATION

What, then, lies ahead in the field of family therapy and its utilization in the treatment of schizophrenia? Perhaps one issue that jumps out of this discussion is the need for better and more careful research that will answer the questions of efficacy and effectiveness within and between models of intervention. Empirical evidence of effectiveness, although still the benchmark for some professionals, should give way to additional methods of evaluating family therapy models with schizophrenia. In some ways, this view of developing research strategies is paradoxical. On the one hand, the profession worries about the lack of empirical evidence to support a number of family therapy models. On the other hand, those models with extensive empirical support have set a high standard that may not be applicable to some of the poorly supported models. Are the mechanisms by which psychoeducational programs get evaluated the same for narrative family therapy? Is empirical support the only support that will carry weight among professionals? Should families coping with schizophrenia only be offered services through models that have extensive empirical support? These are difficult questions to answer. But professionals will need to answer them soon. The use of more and better psychopharmacologic interventions, shorter hospitalizations, increased use of community-based care, and the influence of health maintenance organizations (HMOs) in funding such care, has already reshaped what family therapists working with schizophrenia can do. There is no reason to believe these influences will change in the future.

One way of beginning to answer such questions is to address the need for creativity in the research process. Sprenkle and Moon (1996) raise the issue in their call for pluralism in the research process. But in the area of family work with schizophrenia, it is not just about how you study a phenomena, it is also about what phenomena you study. So much remains unknown about schizophrenia within the context of the family. One look at the family developmental life cycle and you can see myriad different issues that might arise at each stage. Once you factor in gender, ethnicity, and family composition (e.g., single parent, adoptive parent, gay or lesbian parent), the issues grow exponentially. The questions that get raised by looking at the intersection of schizophrenia and family require creativity and flexibility in the research necessary to answer them. Translating the research findings into treatment strategies will require careful work.

One way to address the need for more and better research with a creative twist is to go back to an old issue. The schism that exists between researcher and therapist did not always exist, at least when it comes to family work with schizophrenia. The early pioneers in the field, such as Gregory Bateson and Jay Haley among others, moved easily between the two roles. Although today's researchers might belittle the softness and interpretive nature of their research, and today's clinicians might be concerned about the interference of research in the development of a therapeutic relationship, these practitioner-scientists developed a model of working that still has much merit.

Several years ago I took part on a radio show where the topic was how clinicians are trained to do research. I spoke for the profession of social work, and two other guests, a professor of psychology and a psychoanalyst, spoke for their respective professions. The topic of the show was how each profession trains its practitioners to research the effectiveness of the services provided. Although the psychoanalyst claimed the basic training of psychoanalysis was built on clinicians being researchers through the interpretive analysis of case study data, both the psychologist and myself saw the need for specific training to better equip our professional colleagues with the tools to evaluate the effectiveness of our services.

In the courses on research methodology that I teach, the issue of the practitioner-researcher continues to arise. How can those who do research better communicate with those who primarily practice? How can those who primarily practice get more involved in the research process? How can the dual role of the practitioner-researcher be better supported within professions and better advanced as a model for action to new professionals? The ability of family therapy programs and other professional training programs (e.g., social work and psychology) to address these issues will dictate how well the professions finally put to rest the old dichotomy between practice and research.

Finally, one last issue must be addressed if the field of family therapy is to advance in its work with schizophrenia. How can the professions move the next generation of family therapists closer to working directly with schizophrenia and developing models specific for schizophrenia? Why have so many family therapists essentially abandoned their role in the treatment of schizophrenia? There are no easy answers to these questions. Money, prestige, motivation, needing to realize immediate results, looking for populations with higher profiles and status, may all be part of the answer. But whatever the reason, it remains difficult to encourage students to work with people with schizophrenia on either an individual or family basis. It is even harder to get these students to see the value of such work once they leave their professional training programs. Into this vacuum often comes the less-skilled, less-motivated individual who is asked to do a tremendous amount of work for little pay. Until the professions that train future family clinicians can respond to this concern, the outlook is not promising. Who will be the clinicians of the future? Who will work with people with schizophrenia and their families? What kinds of quality interventions will they have available? We must wait and see.

References

Ackerman, N. (1961). The schizophrenic patient and his family group. In M. Greenblat, D. Levenson, and G. Klerman (Eds.), *Mental patients in transition* (pp. 273-282). Springfield, IL: Charles C Thomas.

Ackerman, N., and Franklin, P. (1965). Family dynamics and the reversibility of delusional formation: A case study in family therapy. In I. Boszormenyi-Nagy and J. Framo (Eds.), *Intensive family therapy: Theoretical and practical aspects* (pp. 245-287). New York: Harper and Row.

Amador, X., and David, A. (Eds.) (1998). *Insight and psychosis*. New York: Oxford University Press.

American Psychiatric Association. (2000). *Diagnostic and statistical manual of mental disorders,* Fourth edition, Text revision. Washington, DC: Author.

Anderson, C., Reiss, D., and Hogarty, G. (1986). *Schizophrenia and the family: A practitioner's guide to psychoeducation and management*. New York: The Guilford Press.

Aponte, H. (1994). *Bread and spirit: Therapy with the new poor: Diversity of race, culture, and values*. New York: Norton.

Boszormenyi-Nagy, I. (1965). Intensive family therapy as process. In I. Boszormenyi-Nagy and J. Framo (Eds.), *Intensive family therapy: Theoretical and practical aspects* (pp. 87-142). New York: Harper and Row.

Boszormenyi-Nagy, I., and Framo, J. (Eds.) (1965). *Intensive family therapy: Theoretical and practical aspects*. New York: Harper and Row.

Bowen, M. (1978). *Family therapy in clinical practice*. Northvale, NJ: Jason Aronson.

Bustillo, J., Lauriello, J., Horan, W., and Keith, S. (2001). The psychosocial treatment of schizophrenia: An update. *American Journal of Psychiatry, 158,* 163-175.

Cole, S., and Cole, D. (1987). Professionals who work with families of the mentally ill: Current status and suggestions for clinical training. In A. Hatfield and H. Lefley (Eds.), *Families of the mentally ill: Coping and adaptation* (pp. 278-306). New York: The Guilford Press.

De Jong, P., and Miller, S. (1995). How to interview for client strengths. *Social Work, 40,* 729-736.

de Shazer, S. (1985). *Keys to solution in brief therapy*. New York: Norton.

de Shazer, S. (1991). *Putting difference to work*. New York: Norton.

de Shazer, S. (1994). *Words were originally magic*. New York: Norton.

Detre, T., Sayer, J., Norton, A., and Lewis, H. (1961). An experimental approach to the treatment of the acutely ill psychiatric patient in the general hospital. *Connecticut Medicine, 25,* 613-619.

Dixon, L., Adams, C., and Lucksted, A. (2000). Update on family psychoeducation for schizophrenia. *Schizophrenia Bulletin, 26,* 5-20.

Dixon, L., and Lehman, A. (1995). Family interventions for schizophrenia. *Schizophrenia Bulletin, 21,* 631-643.

Dixon, L., Stewart, B., Burland, J., Delahanty, J., Lucksted, A., and Hoffman, M. (2001). Pilot study of the effectiveness of the family-to-family education program. *Psychiatric Services, 52,* 965-967.

Dworkin, R. (1992). *Researching persons with mental illness.* Newbury Park, CA: Sage Publications.

Epston, D., and White, M. (1992). *Experience, contradiction, narrative, and imagination: Selected papers of David Epston and Michael White, 1989-1991.* Adelaide, Australia: Dulwich Centre Publications.

Falloon, I., Boyd, J., and McGill, C. (1984). *Family care of schizophrenia.* New York: The Guilford Press.

Falloon, I., and Liberman, R. (1983). Behavioral therapy for families with child management problems. In M. Textor (Ed.), *Helping families with special problems.* New York: Jason Aronson.

First, M., Spitzer, R., Gibbon, M., and Williams, J. (1997). *Structured clinical interview for DSM-IV axis I disorders: Clinician version (SCID-CV).* Washington, DC: American Psychiatric Press, Inc.

Forrest, D. (1976). Nonsense and sense in schizophrenic language. *Schizophrenia Bulletin, 2,* 286-301.

Foucault, M. (1965). *Madness and civilization.* New York: Random House.

Framo, J. (1965). Rationale and techniques of intensive family therapy. In I. Boszormenyi-Nagy and J. Framo (Eds.), *Intensive family therapy: Theoretical and practical aspects* (pp. 143-212). New York: Harper and Row.

Framo, J. (1992). *Family-of-origin therapy: An intergenerational approach.* Northvale, NJ: Jason Aronson.

Gabbard, G. (1994). *Psychodynamic psychiatry in clinical practice: The DSM-IV edition.* Washington, DC: American Psychiatric Press, Inc.

Gerhart, U. (1990). *Caring for the chronic mentally ill.* Itasca, IL: F.E. Peacock Publishers.

Gilman, S. (1985). *Difference and pathology: Stereotypes of sexuality, race, and madness.* Ithaca, NY: Cornell University Press.

Goering, P., Tolomiczenko, G., Sheldon, T., Boydell, K., and Wasylenki, D. (2002). Characteristics of persons who are homeless for the first time. *Psychiatric Services, 53,* 1472-1474.

Gould, S. (2000). *The lying stones of Marrakech: Penultimate reflections in natural history.* New York: Harmony Books.

Greenberg, L., and Johnson, S. (1988). *Emotionally focused therapy for couples.* New York: The Guilford Press.

Grinspoon, L. (Ed.) (1995). Schizophrenia update—Part I and II. *The Harvard Mental Health Letter, 11*(12), 1-4; *12*(1), 1-5.

Grinspoon, L. (Ed.) (1998). New treatments for schizophrenia—Part I and II. *The Harvard Mental Health Letter, 14*(10), 1-3; *14*(11), 1-3.

Guerin, P. (Ed.) (1976). *Family therapy: Theory and practice.* New York: Gardner Press.

Haley, J. (1963). *Strategies of psychotherapy.* New York: Grune and Stratton.

Haley, J. (1987). *Problem-solving therapy,* Second edition. San Francisco: Jossey-Bass.

Langs, R. (1973). *The technique of psychoanalytic psychotherapy* (Vols. 1-2). Northvale, NJ: Jason Aronson.

Lanin-Kettering, I., and Harrow, M. (1985). The thought behind the words: A view of schizophrenic speech and thinking disorders. *Schizophrenia Bulletin, 11,* 1-7.

Laplanche, J., and Pontalis, J.-B. (1973). *The language of psychoanalysis.* New York: Norton.

Laqueur, H., LaBurt, H., and Morong, E. (1964). Multiple family therapy: Further developments. *International Journal of Social Psychiatry, 10,* 69-80.

Leff, J. (2001). *The unbalanced mind.* New York: Columbia University Press.

Leff, J., and Vaughn, C. (1981). The role of maintenance therapy and relatives' expressed emotion in relapse of schizophrenia: A two-year follow up. *British Journal of Psychiatry, 139,* 102-104.

Lehman, A., and Cordray, D. (1993). Prevalence of alcohol, drug, and mental disorders among the homeless: One more time. *Contemporary Drug Problems, 20,* 355-383.

Liberman, R. (Ed.) (1992). *Handbook of psychiatric rehabilitation.* New York: Macmillan Publishing Company.

Lukoff, D., Nuechterlein, K., and Ventura, J. (1986). Manual for the expanded Brief Psychiatric Rating Scale. *Schizophrenia Bulletin, 1,* 594-602.

Madanes, C. (1981). *Strategic family therapy.* San Francisco: Jossey-Bass.

Marley, J. (1992). Content and context: Working with mentally ill people in family therapy. *Social Work, 37,* 412-417.

Marley, J. (1998). People matter: Client-reported interpersonal interaction and its impact on symptoms of schizophrenia. *Social Work, 43,* 437-444.

Marley, J. (1999). Family therapy and schizophrenia: A developing model for practice. *Journal of Family Psychotherapy, 10,* 1-14.

Marley, J., and Buila, S. (1999). When violence happens to people with mental illness: Disclosing victimization. *American Journal of Orthopsychiatry, 69,* 398-402.

Marley, J., and Buila, S. (2001). Crimes against people with mental illness: Types, perpetrators, and influencing factors. *Social Work, 46,* 115-124.

McFarlane, W. (Ed.) (1983). *Family therapy in schizophrenia.* New York: The Guilford Press.

McFarlane, W. (1990). Multiple family groups in the treatment of schizophrenia. In H. Nasrallah (Ed.), *Handbook of schizophrenia* (pp. 167-189). New York: Elsevier.

McFarlane, W. (1995). Families in the treatment of psychotic disorders. *Harvard Mental Health Letter, 12*(4), 4-6.

McFarlane, W. (2002). *Multifamily groups in the treatment of severe psychiatric disorders.* New York: The Guilford Press.

McFarlane, W., and Cunningham, K. (1996). Multiple family groups and psychoeducation: Creating therapeutic social networks. In J. Vaccaro and G. Clark (Eds.), *Practicing psychiatry in the community: A manual* (pp. 387-406). Washington, DC: American Psychiatric Press, Inc.

McGoldrick, M., and Gerson, R. (1985). *Genograms in family assessment.* New York: Norton.

McGoldrick, M., Heiman, M., and Carter, B. (1993). The changing family life cycle: A perspective on normalcy. In F. Walsh (Ed.), *Normal family process,* Second edition (pp. 405-443). New York: The Guilford Press.

Miller, M. (Ed.) (2001). How schizophrenia develops: New evidence and new ideas. *Harvard Mental Health Letter, 17*(8), 1-4.

Minuchin, P., Colapinto, J., and Minuchin, S. (1998). *Working with families of the poor.* New York: The Guilford Press.

Minuchin, S. (1974). *Families and family therapy.* Cambridge, MA: Harvard University Press.

Minuchin, S., Montalvo, B., Guerney, B., Rosman, B., and Schumer, F. (1967). *Families of the slums.* New York: Basic Books.

Minuchin, S., Rosman, B., and Baker, L. (1978). *Psychosomatic families: Anorexia nervosa in context.* Cambridge, MA: Harvard University Press.

Mowbray, C., and Tan, C. (1993). Consumer-operated drop-in centers: Evaluation of operations and impact. *Journal of Mental Health Administration, 20,* 8-19.

Muesur, K., and Glynn, S. (1999). Behavioral family therapy for psychiatric disorders, Second edition. New York: New Harbinger.

Napier, A., and Whitaker, C. (1978). *The family crucible.* New York: Harper and Row.

Neill, J., and Kniskern, D. (Eds.) (1982). *From psyche to system: The evolving therapy of Carl Whitaker.* New York: The Guilford Press.

Nichols, M., and Schwartz, R. (2001). *Family therapy: Concepts and methods,* Fourth edition. Boston: Allyn and Bacon.

Norcross, J., Santrock, J., Campbell, L., Smith, T., Sommer, R., and Zuckerman, E. (2000). *Authoritative guide to self-help resources in mental health.* New York: The Guilford Press.

O'Shea, M., and Phelps, R. (1985). Multiple family therapy: Current status and critical appraisal. *Family Process, 24,* 555-582.

Piercy, F., Sprenkle, D., Wetchler, J., and Associates. (1996). *Family therapy source book,* Second edition. New York: The Guilford Press.

Robbins, M. (1993). *Experiences of schizophrenia: An integration of the personal, scientific, and therapeutic.* New York: The Guilford Press.

Robins, L., and Regier, D. (1991). *Psychiatric disorders in America.* New York: The Free Press.

Rowan, T., and O'Hanlon, B. (1999). *Solution-oriented therapy for chronic and severe mental illness.* New York: John Wiley and Sons.

Rutter, D. (1985). Language in schizophrenia: The structure of monologues and conversations. *British Journal of Psychiatry, 146,* 339-404.

Segal, S., Redman, D., and Silverman, C. (2000). Measuring clients' satisfaction with self-help agencies. *Psychiatric Services, 51,* 1148-1152.

Segal, S., Silverman, C., Temkin, T. (1993). Empowerment and self-help agency practice for people with mental disabilities. *Social Work, 38,* 705-712.

Selvini Palazzoli, M. (1986). Towards a general model of psychotic family games. *Journal of Marital and Family Therapy, 12,* 339-349.

Selvini Palazzoli, M., Boscolo, L., Cecchin, G., and Prata, G. (1978). *Paradox and counterparadox.* New York: Jason Aronson.

Sprenkle, D., and Moon, S. (1996). Toward pluralism in family therapy research. In D. Sprenkle and S. Moon (Eds.), *Research methods in family therapy* (pp. 3-19). New York: The Guilford Press.

Stanton, D., and Todd, T. (1982). *The family therapy of drug abuse and addiction.* New York: The Guilford Press.

Strenlick, A. (1978). Multiple family group therapy: A review of the literature. *Family process,* 307-325.

Sullivan, H. (1974). *Schizophrenia as a human process.* New York: Norton.

Toro, P. (1990). Evaluating professionally operated and self-help programs for the seriously mentally ill. *American Journal of Community Psychology, 18,* 903-907.

Torrey, E. (1997). *Out of the shadows: Confronting America's mental illness crisis.* New York: John Wiley and Sons.

Urban Institute (2000). A new look at homelessness in America. Available from The Urban Institute, 2100 M. Street, N.W., Washington, DC 20037 <www.urban.org>.

Watzlawick, P., Beavin, J., and Jackson, D. (1967). *Pragmatics of human communication.* New York: Norton.

Weiden, P., and Olfson, M. (1995). Cost of relapse in schizophrenia. *Schizophrenia Bulletin, 21,* 419-429.

Whitaker, C. (Ed.) (1958). *Psychotherapy of chronic schizophrenic patients.* Boston: Little, Brown and Company.

Whitaker, C., and Bumberry, W. (1988). *Dancing with the family: A symbolic experiential approach.* New York: Brunner/Mazel.

Whitaker, C., Felder, R., and Warkentin, J. (1965). Countertransference in the family treatment of schizophrenia. In I. Boszormenyi-Nagy and J. Framo (Eds.), *Intensive family therapy: Theoretical and practical aspects* (pp. 323-341). New York: Harper and Row.

Whitaker, C., and Keith, D. (1981). Symbolic-experiential family therapy. In A. Gurman and D. Kniskern (Eds.), *Handbook of family therapy.* New York: Brunner/Mazel.

Whitaker, C., and Ryan, M. (1989). *Midnight musings of family therapist.* New York: Brunner/Mazel.

White, M., and Epston, D. (1990). *Narrative means to therapeutic ends.* New York: Norton.

Wynne, L. (1961). The study of intrafamilial alignments and splits in exploratory family therapy. In N. Ackerman, F. Beatman, and S. Sherman (Eds.), *Exploring the base for family therapy* (pp. 95-115). New York: Family Service Association of America.

Wynne, L. (1965). Some indications and contraindications for exploratory family therapy. In I. Boszormenyi-Nagy and J. Framo (Eds.), *Intensive family therapy: Theoretical and practical aspects* (pp. 289-322). New York: Harper and Row.

Wynne, L., Ryckoff, I., Day, J., and Hirsch, S. (1958). Pseudomutuality in the family relations of schizophrenics. *Psychiatry, 21,* 205-220.

Yanos, P., Primavera, L., and Knight, E. (2001). Consumer-run service participation, recovery of social functioning, and the mediating role of psychological factors. *Psychiatric Services, 52,* 493-500.

Zimmerman, J., and Dickerson, V. (1996). *If problems talked: Adventures in narrative therapy.* New York: The Guilford Press.

Further Reading

Selected Books for Those Who Know Family Therapy but Not Schizophrenia

Birchwood, M., Hallett, S., and Preston, M. (1989). *Schizophrenia: An integrated approach to research and treatment.* New York: New York University Press.

Buckley, P. (Ed.). (1988). *Essential papers on psychosis.* New York: New York University Press.

Cromwell, R., and Snyder, C. (Eds.). (1993). *Schizophrenia: Origins, processes, treatment, and outcome.* New York: Oxford University Press.

Gottesman, I. (1991). *Schizophrenia genesis: The origins of madness.* New York: W.H. Freeman and Company.

Grob, G. (1994). *The mad among us: A history of the care of America's mentally ill.* Cambridge, MA: Harvard University Press.

Howells, J. (1991). *The concept of schizophrenia: Historical perspectives.* Washington, DC: American Psychiatric Press, Inc.

McGlashan, T., and Keats, C. (1989). *Schizophrenia: Treatment process and outcome.* Washington, DC: American Psychiatric Press, Inc.

Torrey, E., Bowler, M., Taylor, E., and Gottesman, I. (1994). *Schizophrenia and manic-depressive disorder.* New York: Basic Books.

Selected Books for Those Who Know Schizophrenia but Not Family Therapy

Becvar, D., and Becvar, R. (1996). *Family therapy: A systemic integration,* Third edition. Boston: Allyn and Bacon.

Framo, J. (1992). *Family-of-origin therapy: An intergenerational approach.* New York: Brunner/Mazel.

Goldenberg, I., and Goldenberg, H. (1996). *Family therapy: An overview,* Fourth edition. New York: Brooks/Cole Publishing Company.

Harway, M. (Ed.). (1996). *Treating the changing family: Handling normative and unusual events.* New York: John Wiley and Sons.

McGoldrick, M., and Gerson, R. (1985). *Genograms in family assessment.* New York: Norton.

McGoldrick, M., Giordano, J., and Pearce, J. (Eds.). (1996). *Ethnicity and family therapy,* Second edition. New York: The Guilford Press.

Nichols, M., and Schwartz, R. (2001). *Family therapy: Concepts and methods,* Fifth edition. Boston: Allyn and Bacon.

Nichols, W., Pace-Nichols, M., Becvar, D., and Napier, A. (Eds.). (2000). *Handbook of family development and intervention.* New York: John Wiley and Sons.

Odell, M., and Campbell, C. (1998). *The practical practice of marriage and family therapy: Things my training supervisor never told me.* Binghamton, NY: The Haworth Press.

Patterson, J., Williams, L., Grauf-Grounds, C., and Chamow, L. (1998). *Essential skills in family therapy.* New York: The Guilford Press.

Piercy, F., Sprenkle, D., Wetchler, J., and Associates (1996). *Family therapy source book,* Second edition. New York: The Guilford Press.

Index